On Distance, Belonging, Isolation and the Quarantined Church of Today

READING AUGUSTINE

Series Editor:

Miles Hollingworth

Reading Augustine presents books that offer personal, nuanced and oftentimes literary readings of Saint Augustine of Hippo. Each time, the idea is to treat Augustine as a spiritual and intellectual icon of the Western tradition, and to read through him to some or other pressing concern of our current day. Or to some enduring issue or theme. In this way, the writers follow the model of Augustine himself, who produced his famous output of words and ideas in active tussle with the world in which he lived. When the series launched, this approach could raise eyebrows, but now that technology and pandemics have brought us into the world and society like never before, and when scholarship is expected to live the same way and responsibly, the series is well-set and thriving.

Volumes in the series:

On Music, Sense, Affect, and Voice, Carol Harrison
On Solitude, Conscience, Love and Our Inner, and Outer Lives, Ron Haflidson
On Creation, Science, Disenchantment, and the Contours of Being and Knowing, Matthew W. Knotts
On Agamben, Arendt, Christianity, and the Dark Arts of Civilization, Peter Iver Kaufman
On Self-Harm, Narcissism, Atonement, and the Vulnerable Christ, David Vincent Meconi
On Faith, Works, Eternity, and the Creatures We Are, André Barbera
On Time, Change, History, and Conversion, Sean Hannan
On Compassion, Healing, Suffering, and the Purpose of the Emotional Life, Susan Wessel
On Consumer Culture, Identity, the Church and the Rhetorics of Delight, Mark Clavier
On Creativity, Liberty, Love and the Beauty of the Law, Todd Breyfogle
On Education, Formation, Citizenship and the Lost Purpose of Learning, Joseph Clair
On Ethics, Politics and Psychology in the Twenty-First Century, John Rist
On God, the Soul, Evil and the Rise of Christianity, John Peter Kenney
On Love, Confession, Surrender and the Moral Self, Ian Clausen
On Memory, Marriage, Tears, and Meditation, Margaret R. Miles
On Mystery, Ineffability, Silence, and Musical Symbolism, Laurence Wuidar

On Distance, Belonging, Isolation and the Quarantined Church of Today

Pablo Irizar

t&tclark
LONDON • NEW YORK • OXFORD • NEW DELHI • SYDNEY

T&T CLARK
Bloomsbury Publishing Plc
50 Bedford Square, London, WC1B 3DP, UK
1385 Broadway, New York, NY 10018, USA
29 Earlsfort Terrace, Dublin 2, Ireland

BLOOMSBURY, T&T CLARK and the T&T Clark logo are trademarks of Bloomsbury Publishing Plc

First published in Great Britain 2022

Copyright © Pablo Irizar, 2022

Pablo Irizar has asserted his right under the Copyright, Designs and Patents Act, 1988, to be identified as Author of this work.

For legal purposes the Acknowledgements on p. xiii constitute an extension of this copyright page.

Cover image © Tetra Images, LLC / Alamy Stock Photo

All rights reserved. No part of this publication may be reproduced or transmitted in any form or by any means, electronic or mechanical, including photocopying, recording, or any information storage or retrieval system, without prior permission in writing from the publishers.

Bloomsbury Publishing Inc does not have any control over, or responsibility for, any third-party websites referred to or in this book. All internet addresses given in this book were correct at the time of going to press. The author and publisher regret any inconvenience caused if addresses have changed or sites have ceased to exist, but can accept no responsibility for any such changes.

A catalogue record for this book is available from the British Library.

Library of Congress Cataloging-in-Publication Data
Names: Irizar, Pablo, author.
Title: On distance, isolation, belonging and the quarantined church of today / Pablo Irizar.
Description: London; New York: T &T Clark, 2022. | Series: Reading Augustine | Includes bibliographical references and index. |
Identifiers: LCCN 2021029008 (print) | LCCN 2021029009 (ebook) | ISBN 9781350269651 (pb) | ISBN 9781350269668 (hb) | ISBN 9781350269675 (epdf) | ISBN 9781350269682 (epub)
Subjects: LCSH: Church. | Social integration–Religious aspects–Christianity. | Belonging (Social psychology) | Augustine, of Hippo, Saint, 354-430.
Classification: LCC BV640 .I75 2022 (print) | LCC BV640 (ebook) | DDC 261–dc23
LC record available at https://lccn.loc.gov/2021029008
LC ebook record available at https://lccn.loc.gov/2021029009

ISBN: HB: 978-1-3502-6966-8
PB: 978-1-3502-6965-1
ePDF: 978-1-3502-6967-5
ePUB: 978-1-3502-6968-2

Series: Reading Augustine

Typeset by Deanta Global Publishing Services, Chennai, India
Printed and bound in Great Britain

To find out more about our authors and books visit www.bloomsbury.com and sign up for our newsletters.

*Daughters of Jerusalem, I adjure you,
By the hinds and the gazelles of the fields
Do not stir nor awaken love
Before He so desires*

Song of Songs 2.7

CONTENTS

Preface viii
Foreword x
Acknowledgements xiii
Notes on texts and translation xv
List of abbreviations xvi

Introduction 1

1   The problem of belonging 9

2   The structure of belonging 37

3   The making of belonging 59

4   The manifestation of belonging 81

5   The metamorphosis of belonging 105

Conclusion 125

Notes 133
References 150
Index 153

PREFACE

This book explores what it means to belong in the church during times of pandemic, distance and isolation. I began shaping my thoughts on Augustine's question of belonging in 2014 as I arrived at KU Leuven for graduate studies in philosophy, and years later as a Research Foundation Flanders – FWO doctoral fellow in theology. As I completed my doctoral research, and as the pandemic progressively reconfigured everyday life and especially the practice of religion in Montreal, I began to reflect on what it means to belong in a quarantined church. According to Catholic teaching, the life of grace depends on the sacraments. How could belief in the necessity of sacraments – to impart and sustain the life of the spirit – which is at the very heart of what it means to belong in the church, abruptly break, for an indeterminate period, because of the pandemic? Are the sacraments not needed the most during times of hardship and as much as during times of joy? Moreover, if sacraments and liturgical obligations can be wavered, as indeed they were by pontifical dispensations, under some circumstances, no matter how dire these may be, they can be then waved under any and every circumstance. These questions arise not from political considerations on social guidelines aiming to cope with the pandemic, nor are these questions about the institutional response of the ecclesial hierarchy to the closure of churches and the dispensation of the sacraments. These questions were foremost theological and philosophical, namely about the purpose of the church in the midst of a pandemic and about the status of the believer in the absence of formal sacramental practice. The questions were about what it means to belong in the church tout court. Drawing from my study of Augustine, I began to consider the relationship between belonging, isolation, distance and quarantine. In March of 2020, soon after the outbreak of the pandemic in Montreal, I started gathering my thoughts systematically in an article which was later awarded the 2020 Louvain Studies Theological Research Award: 'Where Is the Church?' About a year later, my Doktorvater, Anthony Dupont, introduced me to Miles Hollingworth, editor of the series Reading Augustine with Bloomsbury Academic, to discuss the possibility of developing my article into a sustained theological response to the question of belonging in a church in quarantine. From the outset, Miles expressed much enthusiasm for the idea and graciously invited me to work on the article and to draw from my doctoral research to produce a book for the series. Writing this book, in tandem with my responsibilities as director of the Newman Centre, and in addition to my teaching and research responsibilities at the School of Religious Studies of McGill University, proved a demanding and delightful experience thanks to the ongoing encouragement from Miles and Anthony. Alas, on Palm Sunday, the manuscript comes to realization.

Palm Sunday
Oka, Quebec
28 March 2021

FOREWORD

The Covid-19 pandemic that is raging throughout the world today has had a devastating effect that is more than the toll of those who are sick or have died. It has also placed massive stress upon the fabric of society, whether that be family, civil society or the community of the church.

Restrictions made in the interest of fighting the spread of the virus have led to people losing their livelihood, with attendant personal anguish for individuals and for families, and the increased isolation has afflicted us all. By nature, we are social creatures, and we need to belong, but we are forced into unnatural isolation, which can exacerbate the already existing disintegration of society into lonely islands of autonomy.

The negative effect of the increased isolation and the breakdown of natural social interaction is all the more painful in the community of the church, the body of Christ, in which our belonging strengthens our unity of love in the web of relationships, modelled on the relationships of love of the persons of the Trinity, which give us life in a world too often divided. We are sustained by the encounter with Christ in word and sacrament within the sacred liturgy, which is the blessed norm for our life as a community of disciples. In an old hymn I recall from my youth we sang: 'draw us the nearer each to each we plead, by drawing all to thee, O Prince of Peace.' We are accustomed to regular access to the physical experience of our communion with the Lord and with one another when we gather for the liturgy in our parish churches.

Is that fruitful belonging experienced in the church simply lost when the isolation of the pandemic comes down upon us, and the health restrictions limit or at least for a time terminate our access not only to the physical gatherings of the family of faith but also to the sacraments, in which we draw closer to God? Can we experience the belonging which is a fundamental human need when we are physically at a distance from one another? What is the meaning of relationship within the Christian community in a time of pandemic?

These are grievous questions for the people of God. They obviously are made more pressing now because of the pandemic restrictions, which bring them into sharp relief, like a medical dye injected to make more visible the unseen dynamics of the body. But long before the pandemic struck, these questions were already present for Christians facing the onward march of secularism that disintegrates the bonds of unity, an advance made even more destructive because of the dynamics of an omnipresent internet technology that simulates human relationship but actually privileges the creation of lonely islands of autonomy.

Faced with this challenge, made more urgent by the pandemic, we are wise to seek the wisdom of that most humane and passionate saint, the great Augustine, brilliant in intellect and intense in his loving relationship with God and neighbour.

Dr Pablo Irizar, in *Reading Augustine: On Distance, Belonging, Isolation and the Quarantined Church of Today*, offers us insights to help guide us in this present crisis of the pandemic, insights gathered from the world of philosophy but above all from the life and works of Augustine, and from the sources of Christian faith rooted in scripture from which Augustine drew so much. I have always been impressed by Augustine's request to bishop Valerius, upon his ordination, for what we might call a sabbatical so that he could delve more deeply into the riches of scripture. Natural intellectual brilliance, classical philosophical and rhetorical education, practical pastoral experience, a life of friendship and Christian community, and a profound knowledge of the Word of God all come together in Augustine to make his insights as relevant today as they were in his own age. Dr Irizar's profound knowledge of Augustine, made fruitful not only through his great learning but also through his own life of discipleship, offers us a most valuable analysis of the challenges faced by Christians today as they seek to make present on earth the love of the persons of the Trinity.

It is particularly pertinent to reflect on what is meant by belonging. If we consider our belonging within the community of the church from a merely human or organizational perspective, then the organizational restrictions of the pandemic, imposed by governments and health officials, can indeed fill us with alarm. How can we experience belonging if we are kept apart? The physical church may be closed for an extended period, and access to the sacraments restricted. Of course, we of North America and Europe may forget that for many if not most of our brothers and sisters in Christ in other parts of the world, such denial of the sacraments or of the opportunity to come together physically in community is common for reasons such as distance, persecution and war. But Augustine helps us to realize that our human relationships, and our life as church, are ultimately rooted in the relationships of generous love among the divine persons of the Blessed Trinity. And we are one in Christ crucified. Organizational impediments of whatever character cannot overcome that basic reality, which gives us hope as we journey through this valley of tears, homeward bound for that ultimate community, our true home, the heavenly Jerusalem.

Augustine shows us the significance of a deep understanding of belonging to the vision of humanity found in the Psalms, interpreted in the context of Christ. His meditation on the seven words of Christ from the cross illuminates our own experience, as does his reflection on Christ, sharing our human affliction through his sacrifice on the cross, and manifest in the body of Christ which is the church. Augustine's sublime insights into time and eternity can guide us now as we seek to situate our present crisis of disorienting separation within the plan of God.

As a bishop of a large diocese, facing the unexpected struggles precipitated so suddenly by the pandemic, while already seeking ways to make our Christian community an oasis of Trinitarian life in the expanding sterile desert of secular autonomy, I greatly appreciate Dr Irizar's reflections on the wisdom which Augustine offers, and which in his writings is so fully rooted in the words of Sacred Scripture, and in the personal encounter with Christ which is fundamental for the life of discipleship. I never forget that in addition to being a towering figure of spiritual wisdom for the ages, Augustine was a working bishop who did all his writing while tending to the practical pastoral cares of a diocese caught up in the turmoil of heresy, civil strife, ecclesial contention and barbarian invasion. Our problems seem tame compared to that. We owe a debt of gratitude to Dr Irizar for sharing with us in our current crisis the sublime and ever relevant wisdom of Saint Augustine.

Thomas Cardinal Collins
Archbishop of Toronto
Toronto, Canada
1 May 2021

ACKNOWLEDGEMENTS

For many, Easter 2020 never came. Many more eagerly await Easter 2021. After a yearlong Lent, and as the Easter of deconfinement draws near, this manuscript fittingly comes to realization. The labour of writing is a labour of asceticism: the labour of silence, daily persistence, consistency, sacrifice, recollection, precision and self-denial. The labour of writing is also, and mainly, the labour of love. I mean not the love of writing but the loving labour of those who make the obsessive discipline of study a possible and pleasant reality. I remain ever grateful to all of those with whose gracious love, support and sacrifice, at times even unknowingly, I have persevered in this undertaking. This work is a testament to their abundant sacrifices; it is the ink spilled on every margin. Foremost gratitude is due to my Doktorvater Anthony Dupont, professor of Christian Antiquity at KU Leuven. As I walked along the Naamsestraat early upon my arrival at Leuven years ago, a friend suggested that I join a Latin Patristics course dedicated to Augustine. Dissatisfied with a purely philosophical analysis of the towering North African figure, I immediately obliged and joined the seminar where I met Anthony for the first time. This experience changed the course of my academic trajectory, as shortly thereafter I began to prepare a doctoral project under Anthony's supervision. Thank you, Anthony, for believing in my work, for your support, for guiding me along the way with wisdom, patience and resolve. Like Augustine, Anthony taught me in word and deed the value of taming intellectual curiosity with the discipline of the mind and spirit. I remain ever grateful for the formative time I enjoyed at the Faculty of Theology and Religious Studies. The memorable Friday luncheons and late afternoon beers at the Oude Markt capture the collegial spirit of the Faculty. I am grateful for the places and people that paved the days of my early journey at Leuven, especially at the American College and at the Hoger Instituut Voor Wijsbegeerte. I am glad to call KU Leuven my intellectual home. Leuven shall remain an important point of reference in years to come. I am also grateful for the gracious financial support of the FWO Research Foundation – Flanders. Without it, I would not have pursued academic research. Furthermore, my thoughts were slowly shaped by the places and people I met along the way in France, Poland, Finland, Italy and throughout Europe and North America. I am deeply grateful to Miles Hollingworth for accepting to publish my manuscript in his series Reading Augustine. Miles has offered timely support and advice along the way, making this experience incredibly pleasant. I am grateful for his professionalism, for his love of Augustine and for his kindness. Utmost gratitude is also due to Thomas Cardinal Collins, who, having witnessed my academic and human development over the years (since 2003 to be precise) accepted – despite his many engagements in Toronto – to read the manuscript and to write a compelling and beautiful foreword. For the gift of life and for the gift of unconditional love, I remain ever grateful to my family, especially to Dolores, Miguel and Juan. Finally, gratitude is foremost due to my wife and her hospitable family. Augustine's prayer of gratitude and contrition in remembrance inspired and sustained the writing process: 'O my God, let me remember with gratitude and confess to thee thy mercies toward me' (*conf.* 8.1).

TEXTS AND TRANSLATIONS

English translations of Augustine's oeuvre are mainly from the Works of Saint Augustine (WSA) by New City Press. For *Confessions*, the translation by Thomas Williams (2019) is preferred, and for *The City of God against the Pagans*, R. W. Dyson's (1988) Cambridge translation is used. Stephen McKenna's *On the Trinity* (1970) is also used. For *The Soliloquies*, Rose E. Cleveland's translation (1910) is used and at times that of John H. S. *Burleigh* (1956). The Latin editions consulted are Jacques-Paul Migne's *Patrologia Latina* (PL) and the *Corpus Christianorum Series Latina* (CCSL). A brief citation from the biography of Augustine *Sancti Augustini Uita* is taken from Herbert T. Weiskotten's translation (1919). The Nicene and Post Nicene Fathers (NPNF) collection and the Fathers of the Church (FC) collection were consulted at times. All biblical citations follow the *English Standard Version* (ESV).

ABBREVIATIONS

Acad.	*Contra academicos*
ciu.	*De ciuitate Dei*
conf.	*Confessiones*
diu. qu.	*De diuersis quaestionibus octaginta tribus*
en. Ps.	*Enarrationes in Psalmos*
ep. Io. tr.	*Tractatus in epistolam Ioannis ad Parthos*
Gn. adu. Man.	*De Genesis aduersus Manichaeos*
Gn. litt.	*De Genesis ad litteram*
Gn. litt. inp.	*De Genesis ad litteram inperfectus*
Io. eu. tr.	*In euangelium Ioannis tractatus*
mor.	*De moribus ecclesiae catholicae et de morbius Manichaeorum*
retr.	*Retractationes*
s.	*Sermones*
sol.	*Soliloquiorium*
spir. et. litt.	*De spiritu et littera*
trin.	*De Trinitate*
FC	*Fathers of the Church*
PL	*Patrologia Latina*
CSEL	*Corpus Christianorum Ecclesiasticorum Latinorum*

CCL	*Corpus Christianorum*
NPNF	Nicene and Post-Nicene Fathers
WSA	*Works of Saint Augustine*
ESV	English Standard Version

Introduction[1]

The ringing bells of deserted churches across Montreal, and indeed around the world, during the quarantine, ongoing for well over a year now, bear unsettling similarities to Nietzsche's requiem for God in 'The Madman'.[2] Together, we ask, 'Whither is God?' What is this great deed of God's death foretold, and do we betray our collective guilt in the stains of silence's blood and in the comforting helplessness of quarantine and isolation? Is the world not spinning out of control? Has it not been spinning out of control since the pandemic broke out? For nearly a year now, hallow churches have stood as hollow gravestones, resounding empty echoes of the communities that once worshipped therein. Meanwhile, the faithful roam helplessly like the madman, looking for a place to worship God. However, where is God, if not in the church? The closure of churches over the weeks and months following the outbreak of the pandemic reduced the faithful to adopt the posture of the madman and to relentlessly seek God even in the marketplace. Quarantine left the world athirst for God, with an insatiable void of loneliness and solitude too great to subdue with a vague promise of deconfinement. Empty churches stood as tombstones all around. These powerful symbols of desolation and isolation raise important questions: How has the quarantine affected the church? When churches lock down and the faithful can no longer congregate to worship, what does it mean to belong in the communion of the church? Has the church dissipated? Furthermore, social distancing has disincarnated the sacraments and virtualized the liturgy, leading some to contest that there is no church in the absence of a community of worship, and thereby inspiring others to advocate for solidarity as the only sure antidote to the agony of solitude.

Gregory Solari notes in an influential piece: 'We want to be united "in solidarity". In solidarity with the sick, with affected families, with a suffering world. In solidarity, even when all social contact is forbidden, as it is today – in solidarity against all odds, from a distance. We want to be united in solidarity even when solidarity is possible only as a discourse.'³ Distance distresses the community of the faithful because, notwithstanding the desire to manifest unity in solidarity, physical absence frustrates every sentiment of goodwill. Solari thus complains that there is no solidarity without a physical community: 'The communion "of desire" nourishes solidarity, which is fed from a distance by Masses diffused online on the sites of our Churches. In solidarity, doubly so, with those who cannot habitually receive communion, and solidarity with the priests who can receive daily communion, in celebrations with otherwise virtual communities only.'⁴ In the absence of presence, the hierarchical church is responsible for bridging the distance in order to ensure the faithful partake in the graces of the sacraments. Solari thus vehemently regrets the distance, which, as he sees it, bifurcates the clerics from the people of God.

> Therefore, why, in these conditions, rather than keeping the baptized at a distance, and thus retaining an archaic image of the Church, with its bipartition – why not take advantage of this confinement to entrust the Eucharist to the baptized faithful, to the families who desire it? Why not take advantage of this confinement to accord responsibility to the baptized rather than maintaining them in this passive posture with regard to pastors and to a pastoral ministry thought out by and ultimately for the pastors? A little consistency: one cannot on the one hand, sing the praises of the 'People of God', go on about the dignity of the baptized, defend the beauty of the family, Christian or otherwise, and concurrently refuse to allow Christian homes to become small domestic churches – *Ecclesiolas*. Can one imagine the 'weight of grace' that this would constitute for the many families who would welcome the Eucharist and thus find strength in the violence of trial, thereby offering numerous resting places in the heart of the world, of the neighborhoods, of the countryside, and no longer in the solitude of a locked church?⁵

According to Solari, the dependence on consecrated priests to minister the sacraments and the unwillingness to confide the Eucharist to the care of the faithful in the domestic homes during confinement betray an outdated ecclesiology at best – where the baptismal priesthood of the faithful remains wanting – or incoherent hypocrisy at worst – where theological categories only pay lip service to the role of the laity in the church. Many around the world understandably share Solari's concerns, which reaffirm the belief in the presence of Christ in the Eucharist coupled with a thirst to find refuge in the sacraments in the midst of troubled times. Yet notwithstanding a seemingly reasonable concern, and at the risk of offering an easy fix to complex questions, underlying Solari's proposal for an ecclesial aggiornamento abound deep questions about the nature of the church and what it means to belong in the community of the faithful during quarantine, distance and isolation. Belonging is a crucial ingredient for human flourishing, yet like most basic requirements for life, it is often taken for granted. However, does social distance really undermine the unity of the church as Solari suggests? Or rather, does social distance offer an opportunity to reconsider the centrality of suffering in the dynamic of church belonging and in the formation of community irrespective of distance? This book draws from the thought of Augustine to argue, against Solari, that distance does not impede belonging and communion. On the contrary, physical distance is an external reminder of the interior fragmentation of human existence aching for wholesomeness, constantly seeking union with the church through the redemptive and performative sufferings of Christ. For Augustine, the community of the church transcends place, and (meaningful) suffering is central to effecting authentic belonging. Belonging for Augustine is about recognizing and contending with interior distance, and about integrating it as a wholesome tapestry of Trinitarian relation in the manifestation of the community of the church in spite of distance. Augustine vouches for the primacy of sight over the incredulity of touch irrespective of presence and absence in the dynamic of belonging in a quarantined church. Sight offers presence irrespective of distance, whereas touch depends on the reach of presence and fails to bridge the rift of absence.

Though Augustine never experienced a pandemic, comparable turmoil in his day prompted him to wrestle with questions of belonging in the church, most notably after the sacking of Rome on 24 August 410 by Alaric. Augustine, as ever, found in crisis a fertile locus for reflection and insight in light of scripture. From the time of his conversion, when Augustine movingly describes scripture as the arrows of God's love, to his prayer of the Psalms on his deathbed, Augustine consistently turned to the Word of God for insight in the midst of adversity. Addressing God in the *Confessions*, Augustine writes, 'you pierced my heart with your word, and I fell in love with you.'[6] This echoes the moment of conversion when a voice in the garden exhorts a restless talented rhetorician to 'Pick up and read, pick up and read'.[7] Augustine's biographer Possidius recounts how Augustine turned to scripture as the sole companion before death:

> For [Augustine] commanded that the shortest penitential Psalms of David should be copied for him, and during the days of his sickness as he lay in bed he would look at these sheets as they hung upon the wall and read them; and he wept freely and constantly. And that his attention might not be interrupted by anyone, about ten days before he departed from the body he asked of us who were present that no one should come in to him, except only at the hours in which the physicians came to examine him or when nourishment was brought to him. This, accordingly, was observed and done, and he had all that time free for prayer. Up to the very moment of his last illness he preached the Word of God in the church incessantly, vigorously and powerfully, with a clear mind and sound judgment.[8]

The Word of God was the thread weaving the fabric of Augustine's life and thought, especially with regard to articulating and addressing what it means to belong. Belonging was, for Augustine, not simply a question of speculation – although this was also the case, and more so with time – but primarily a lived reality. This reality was an existential fissure, from whence progressively emerged an understanding of belonging in terms of alterity. Augustine was ever caught between heaven and earth, the *saeculum* and church, body and soul, living as a pilgrim exile, on the way to the celestial home. This became, for the bishop of Hippo, the problem of belonging, and the human condition was defined as longing to be or be-longing, while always remaining incomplete. Upon studying Paul, after his ordination, the North African presbyter's experience resonated in the words 'the spirit is willing, but the flesh is weak'.[9] This is an experience of division, interior separation and strife. In *Confessions*, after discovering the wisdom of Cicero's *Hortensius* Augustine would pray to God: 'Give me chastity and continence: but not yet.'[10] Again, in an infamous line precipitating the Pelagian controversy, Augustine again would pray, 'command what you will, but give what you command'.[11] Thus, life's enigma best captures the paradoxical state of humanity, 'a life that dies, a death that lives'.[12] For this reason, Augustine writes that upon introspection, 'I have become a question to myself.'[13] Belonging is a question unto itself. Augustine notes, 'there is something in each of us that not even the human spirit within us knows.'[14] In the pandemic, also, encountering solitude in quarantine, as a quarantined church, in distance, is a reminder of our interiorly fragmented, fissured humanity. Augustine's engagement with the problem of belonging is therefore illuminating for our times of turmoil, distance and intensified sense of willing be-longing.

The problem of belonging, for Augustine, is a problem of existential distance, distance from oneself, from others and ultimately from God. Be-longing is about discovering di-stance as the human condition and about the realization in the praise, repentance and belief of confession that God is 'more deeply within me than the innermost part of my being'[15] and that God is the hiddenness 'in each of us that not even the human spirit within us knows'.[16] This is not a helpless resignation to the inevitability of solitude and the search for authenticity therein, as the French existentialists did not tire to suggest in the twentieth century, nor about a Marxist material dialectic and alienation, nor again about the phenomenological nameless and infinite Otherness. The discovery of alterity, for Augustine, is only the beginning of an arduous and exciting journey towards contending with difference and separation in the hope of achieving a wholesome identity. As the young Augustine flirted with the Manichean sect, which he first encountered during his studies in Carthage, a place he later remembers as the frying pan filled with the 'noisy bubbling and sizzling of disgraceful loves'.[17] The Manicheans preached a dualistic world view, which, coupled with the unwillingness to contend with the demands of free will, resonated finely with the young Augustine's experience of existential fissure. However, the eternal strife of opposites in the Manichean cosmogony, the disdain for the body, unrealistic demands and the hypocrisy of its preachers soon ascertained insufficient to address the demands of belonging. Accepting an alien and irreconcilable force within as the alterity of identity, as the Manicheans believed, was out of tune with reality and hardly quietened the inquietude of the soul. Only the journey to God, and God as the subject of human love alone, could do this, as the monumental opening words of *Confessions* memorably enunciate a return to love foretold: 'for you have made us for yourself, and our heart is restless until it comes to rest in you.'[18] The distance of the quarantine functions as a mirror of humanity and is accordingly an external reminder of interiorly constitutive fragmentation, of the longing to *be* and of the inherent nostalgia for homecoming. Di-stance, as interior alterity, finds rest only in fully actualizing an integrative identity. For this, the discovery of the Christian God as the self-same (*idipsum*) in the revelation of God to Moses as 'I am whom am'[19] became for Augustine the model to imitate, the guiding rod to think about and live out belonging. The conceptual framework to understand identity as self-sameness suited well the idea of the One in the 'books of the Platonists'[20] he first encountered in the circle of the Milanese philosophers, including Bishop Ambrose – at whose hand Augustine was eventually received into the church at the age of thirty-three on Easter of 387. However, this was not without major difficulties. Framing identity in terms of a spectrum of likeness towards or away from the Oneness of belonging inevitably implies discarding alterity in the process, for there to be one means, necessarily, that there is no separation in difference. Augustine later revisits this position and reinterprets human belonging in light of Trinitarian alterity, where difference of persons and sameness of divinity harmonize in the divine mystery of God. Augustine thus not only discovers the centrality of alterity in positing the problem of belonging but also locates it as the very structure of what it means to belong. From this vantage point, contending with the difficult demands of a socially distanced and quarantined church translates into contending with the triadic alterity of human identity and into attempting to harmonize difference and sameness within the interplay of alterity. Thus arises the possibility of making belonging from a distance. Wanting 'to make the truth',[21] as Augustine prays in the *Confessions*, consists in labouring to make belonging, not simply as a postulate of conceptual demands, but primarily in the rightful worship of the true God. Piety (εὐσέβεια) is for Augustine about rendering society's due unto God; thus, a just society assembles in rightful praise and worship: 'for a just society is one that serves [God].'[22] Augustine formulates the making of belonging according to the practice of religion in the harmonious praise of the Psalms as church. The Psalms make belonging, for the prayer of the church overcomes the separation of distance in the one voice of Christ, which is the voice of the Psalms before the incarnation. Especially in the expression of suffering in the words of the Psalms, the quarantined church dissipated throughout the world groans as one as the body of Christ. Thus, the alterity of belonging is united in the body of

Christ in spite of distance. The problem of belonging is not primarily about distance but about perception and about the passage from invisibility into the manifestation of presence. In the midst of the suspicion of invisible pathogen and its deadly force, invisibility is mistakenly conflated with the absence of distance of the quarantined church. The problem of belonging, for Augustine, is therefore not about distance, or at least nor primarily, but about gazing anew and about understanding the radicality of invisibility. Quite literally, invisibility roots (*radix*) all reality and, for this reason, the invisibility of distance is not a hindrance to belonging but the space wherein belonging sprouts manifestation. Augustine poignantly notes in an unprecedented formulation of a defining ontological principle of reality, inspired after the figure of the cross, that 'from the depth which you cannot see rises everything that you can see'.[23] The antidote to the invisibility of distance, which again is not absence, is thus about manifesting the constitutive alterity of belonging in the community as church. What is required, henceforth, is not simply overcoming distance but gazing anew and about discovering the transformative and indeed the metamorphosing power of God's creative eye. God grounds the metamorphosing passage from invisibility into the horizon of manifestation, by means of the incarnation, where God is neither only word, nor only flesh but the becoming of the invisible word manifested in the flesh. Augustine's performative paradigm of belonging consists in the creative becoming of the divine gaze. Consequently, the itinerary of de-confinement consists in learning to see anew. We see anew by appreciating that belonging is a process of transformation, a process of becoming something new in the gaze of God. To be, for Augustine, is to be perceived by God. He writes, 'so we see things [God has] made because they are, but they are because [God sees] them'.[24]

The distance and isolation of a church in quarantine has offered an opportunity to appreciate anew the church as a community in the process of transformative manifestation, where the body of Christ is diffused throughout the earth while remaining mysteriously united in suffering and longing during the pandemic and thereafter, until the end of times. Belonging to the church does not require overcoming a physical distance, which Solari regrets voicing the restlessness of many. Belonging is about discovering the existential distance and the longing to be, which Christ has overcome for all times in the church. What is required is to focus on the resurrection, not primarily or only as presence but as transformation: a call to dwell anew as the Easter of deconfinement approaches. Easter is an invitation to see anew. The silence of the Nietzsche's madman is not a silence of resignation; it is a silence that gives way to the primacy of the creative gaze of God, where the invisibility of the spirit enjoins the manifestation of the body as church in spite of isolation, distance and suffering. Construed as an idol of belonging and solely in terms of activist solidarity, the church has truly died in the pandemic. As an icon of God's salvific work, however, the stone graveyards throughout the city yield to the living encounter with Christ. This is the promise of Easter: on the road to Emmaus, accompanied by the incredulity of Thomas, the disciples did not recognize the resurrected Christ. Unlike Thomas, after the pandemic, we will not be able touch that we may believe – touch has been lost and will recover only slowly, in the course of time.[25] Only a purified gaze will remind us that we are the church, and that we have been church all along in spite of the quarantine's distance. 'Lord, let me recover my sight.'[26]

1

The problem of belonging

To understand what it means to belong in the absence of church, and to determine whether this is possible at all, the first step is to understand what it means to belong tout court, and what absence makes of the human longing to be, of be-longing. We intuitively consider presence as an essential requirement of belonging. We belong where we are. After all, we are beings 'of flesh and bones',[1] and thus we are only in the places and spaces that surround, contain and define us. According to this view, since distance is perhaps the most obvious aspect of absence, it is not possible to be present in absence. This means upon first inspection that belonging from a physical distance is not possible. Considered as a metaphor for difference, however, distance suddenly becomes an inescapable aspect of belonging. This does not mean difference is necessary for belonging, but simply that difference is something to contend with in the making of belonging. On this point, the question arises, does distance frustrate belonging and is belonging from a distance possible? In other words, what is the relationship between difference and identity? Upon closer inspection, therefore, belonging – the interplay and rupture of being in longing and the longing to be – poses the problem of identity in terms of difference. The problem of identity is a question of dealing with difference and of reconciling, integrating or overcoming difference in sameness. Augustine understood well that difference is not antagonistic to identity but an inherent part of it. This reflection establishes that belonging in the church in times of pandemic and isolation is not about overcoming social distancing, or at least not primarily. Conversely, confinement is not only about physical separation. Quite on the contrary, distancing is a reminder of the difference integral to human identity and, by consequence, integral to the deep longing to being and becoming. In this sense, social distancing is a reminder of what it means to belong and of the place of belonging in unravelling the enigma of human identity. Distance is therefore not a hindrance to the actualization of presence. On the contrary, distance as difference is a condition for belonging. Identity and belonging in the absence of presence is not only possible but also the starting point of the human predicament and its itinerary towards the de-confining the truth of humanity as constitutive alterity.

Dyadic alterity

Augustine articulates the problem of identity in terms of images and in terms of the source of an image. He particularly insists on understanding how the difference and likeness of an image relate to their source. Consequently, for Augustine, the difference of an image and its likeness corresponds to an inherently divided human identity. Therefore, although human beings seek an existential unifying thread, only by looking beyond themselves is it possible to grasp the core of belonging. Specifically, identity formation consists of integrating the difference of the projected, objectified self-image or the reflection into the source of the image or the idealized subjectified self-same image. In other words, identity depends on integrating difference and sameness in the interplay of alterity. This assumes, naturally, that such integration is possible at all. However, for Augustine, it is not. Difference is irreducible to sameness and sameness resists differentiation. This gives rise to the paradoxes of alterity. In the paradox of alterity, the dynamism of difference and sameness gives rise to identity. Accordingly, the problem of belonging consists in integrating the paradoxes of alterity in identity and in preserving the interplay of difference and sameness. Failure to do so results in the entanglement of the shadows of the imagination, idolatrizing the false images of the self. In confusing the source of our images for the image itself, identity is reduced to either sameness or difference. At stake in facing our own existence in the midst of isolation during the pandemic, mainly because of distance, is the collapse of all points of reference, foregoing self-determination and ultimately failing to achieve authentic identity. Thus, to ask whether belonging is possible in the absence of presence is to ask what difference makes of us at a distance. Specifically, how do difference and sameness interact in identity? Must difference come at the expense of unity, or conversely, is the promise of identity forgone to safeguard difference? Again, is it possible to harmonize, even integrate, the interplay of alterity within identity, such that difference and sameness constitute an inherent whole? Corresponding to these questions are three responses. These are: (1) totalizing sameness, (2) absolutizing difference and (3) integrating sameness and difference within the dynamism of alterity.[2] According to the first two models, identity is static and clearly predetermined. That is to say, in totalizing sameness and absolutizing difference, identity is either about unity in sameness or, in the second case, about difference without a common denominator. The first relies on determination by means of rejection of difference, while the second focuses on indetermination by means of affirmation of sameness. Alternatively, the third model attempts to harmonize or even to integrate the interplay of difference and sameness into identity. Augustine follows and develops the third model. However, Augustine articulates this model only as his thought progressed and as he continued to integrate his experience as a young rhetorician, and later as a priest, bishop, pastor and speculative thinker.

That the notion of image proved for Augustine a useful tool to conceptualized identity is not surprising particularly because of what images denoted during his time. Some of these reasons are obvious. For example, even today, to the extent that images represent (something about) who we are, that is, to the extent we identify to them, images capture identity. In Augustine's language, images are signs or traces of the thing they signify.[3] Within Augustine's cultural context, images of the emperor, for instance, secured the power of the monarch in absentia. This means that images not only represent but also in a sense have the power to conjure a presence and even to command a corresponding authority and respect. This is not far-fetched when we think about the image of a loved one on the wall or on our desk. They are reminders of the person they represent and somehow command respect based on who they are to us. For this reason, we would not stump (at least not deliberately) on the picture of our wife or husband, for instance. Similarly, the sculpted images of deities in the Pantheon commanded respect. A Roman practice consisted of enduring the memory and presence of a deceased ancestor by means of displaying their image in the atrium or family garden. Images also denoted for Augustine something ambivalent. Masks were images used in Greek theatre to represent a face or person (πρόσωπον), which the actor would adopt for a performance. In other words, the mask was a tool for personification. Thus, images on masks were means of deceitfulness, concealment, uncertainty and ambivalence. Finally, images were inherent to the life of worship in Antiquity. After all, the prevalent popular understanding of deity, even in North African Christian circles, was a material one.[4] That gods were material, even the Christian God, warranted their depictions for veneration. This sparked much controversy in the seventeenth century called iconoclasm, where some contested the possibility of iconic signification and argued accordingly against the legitimacy of images as idols. The legitimacy of images and their incarnational function was championed by the likes of John Damascène, who wrote in the aftermath of iconoclasm:

> I do not venerate matter, but the Creator of matter, who *became matter for my sake* and deigned *to live in matter* and bring about my salvation through matter. I will not cease therefore to venerate matter through which my salvation was achieved. But I do not venerate it in absolute terms as God! [. . .] *Do not, therefore, offend matter*: it is not contemptible, because nothing that God has made is contemptible.[5]

These varied notions and functions related to images – representation, signification, remembrance, worship, corporeality, presence and ambivalence – are central to thinking about identity.

For these reasons, it was easy for Augustine, based on his cultural milieu, to adopt the rich symbolism of images as a ready tool to capture and conceptualize questions of identity. Moreover, the rich symbolic import of the notion of image to conceptualize identity fitted quite well in light of Augustine's exposure and commitment to Platonist philosophies, his later biblical study and reading of the letters of Paul and, most importantly, in view of Augustine's tireless and impressive efforts to harmonize faith, culture and philosophy. In his early days of conversion, intellectual and spiritual, the unrefined language of the Bible proved a stumbling obstacle for the talented young professor of rhetoric in Milan. Compared to the eloquence and elegance of the Roman poets, Augustine complains in the *Confessions*, the Bible clearly could not bear a message of truth. Eventually, Augustine came to understand that there is eloquence in humility also, and that the simplicity of scripture was an antidote to the pride of life. Augustine would then embrace the humility of truth found in the love of God, neighbour and self, as an alternative path to the restless and reckless thirst for the power of persuasion. However, in his youth, Augustine found the Bible too unsophisticated for his taste. This was the fruit of much spiritual and intellectual labour, however. As a youngster flirting with new ideas in Carthage, the young North African turned to Manicheanism, a gnostic religion founded by Mani in Persia, for answers instead. Augustine quickly adopted the Manichean ridicule of the creation story in Genesis, for instance. Indeed, one of the arguments for discarding the Old Testament and its conception of God was the incredulity of the creation story, particularly the claim that human beings were fashioned according to the image and likeness of God (Gen. 1.26). The problem was not only one of cosmogony – the narrative of the world's origin – but primarily one of theology – what does the creation story reveals about its creator, about God – and of philosophy – for the search of wisdom in Antiquity was not divorced from a practical commitment to a way of life. The Manichean dualistic ontology, according to which all things spiritual are good and all things material are evil, required that a good God be void of materiality. Thus, the Manicheans would reason, if human beings somehow resemble God, by implication God too must somehow resemble humans. However, God can resemble humans only in that humans are material, because God is by nature spiritual. Thus, to say human beings resemble God implies God is material. Since matter is evil, then God must be evil. Therefore, the Manicheans reasoned, human beings cannot resemble God. Following this line of thought, which depends on a dualistic ontology, Augustine struggled to reconcile materiality and the idea that humans have a divine likeness. How this was possible, however, without anthropomorphizing the gods on the one hand, or without divinizing human beings on the other hand, Augustine articulated only later in terms of a non-dualistic Platonic ontology of image. Augustine begins to wrestle with the problem of identity by articulating human identity as the image of God in terms of a Plotinian image ontology. The convergence of an image ontology and the interpretation of Gen. 1.26, humanity's divine image and likeness, begins in Augustine's earliest extant writings, when he was around thirty-three years old. There, the foreground to the question of identity is not one of ontology, however, but a question of determining the truth of things and, specifically, the truth of images in perception. Identity begins as a question of truth and of falsehood. According to a school of philosophy in Late Antiquity called the Sceptics or Academics, since nothing from perception can be determined with certainty, the only attitude appropriate to the seeker of wisdom consists in suspending judgement by acquiring equipollence. Equipollence means equal power. The equal power of persuasion in considering a thesis and its antithesis would inevitably result, upon conducting an honest assessment, in suspending judgement. This, in turn, would produce peace of mind, free from disturbances (ἀταραξία). This was the sceptic's antidote to the restlessness of upholding a proposition in the absence of complete certainty. After all, philosophy was not about theoretical speculation but about a way of life and the search for happiness. For the sceptic, happiness consisted in achieving peace of mind. In arriving at this approach to life and reality, the chief consideration for the sceptic consisted in noting the unreliability of sense perception. The images of perception (φαντασίαι) that the senses yield, and which is the basis for making judgements, is unreliable. The senses are prone to distortion of sensual contingencies. Thus if the images obtained by sense perception are potentially faulty, how is it possible to draw conclusions about reality based on them? More importantly, how can the most important question of all, namely how to live a good and happy life, depend on flimsy sense perception? This problem leads the sceptic to the inevitable question, what is the criterion of truth and is the truth of images possible at all? The sceptic was not interested in finding an Archimedean point to build a sure system of knowledge, as was the case centuries later for Descartes. For the sceptic, the mistrust of the senses was part of a larger methodical attitude and practice of life. By acknowledging the unreliability of images and their ambivalent character in sense perception, the sceptic recommended suspending judgement. Although at one point in his life, soon after parting ways with the Manicheans, Augustine adopts scepticism, he later found in Platonism a powerful system to secure the truth of images. In other words, thanks to the Platonic ontology, images not only were inherently ambivalent outcomes of sense perception but could, due to their inherent volatility, which was in turn captured by a rich spectrum of likeness, account for truth, falsehood and dynamic resemblance. Augustine learnt about the ontology of images through Ambrose, at whose hand Augustine received baptism. Ambrose and the 'books of the Platonists'[6] in Milan taught Augustine that error in perception is due to judgement, not sensation, and that images are not only a static, material and unreliable entity but complex and dynamic, immaterial and objects of signification. Thus, there was a major shift in considering images from a question of perception, or epistemology, to a question of the constitution of reality, or ontology and metaphysics. This afforded Augustine the tools to interpret the truth of human identity and its falsehood also, in terms of a likeness to the divine image as per Gen. 1.26. However, eventually, Platonism would commit Augustine to a dyadic treatment of alterity, which, though initially proved expedient, even to inspire his conversion, would later require reconsideration in light of the Trinity. This was only years later.

How does Augustine first encounter the Platonic ontology of images? The earliest traces of Augustine's commitment to a Platonic ontology of image and the discovery of its rich import to consider identity appear in an early dialogue called the *Soliloquy*, composed around 386. In it, Augustine defines the notion of identity as the truth of images. 'If, then, [images] were true by reason of their appearing perfectly similar to the true, so that nothing whatever differentiates them from the true, and false by reason of corresponding or other differences, must it not be admitted also that similitude is the mother of Truth and dissimilitude of Falisty?'[7] This rich passage presents two defining characteristics of images for Augustine. First, images, considered not only culturally but now also ontologically, can be deceitful in representation. For this reason, Augustine spent much time thinking about how to distinguish an image from reality. To explore this question, he explores a number of scenarios. Four examples recur often. First, the comparisons of two eggs, which appear similar but are different. This illustrates similarity does not imply equality. Second, Augustine notes that dreams resemble reality. However, when awake, it is clear that dreams are not reality; otherwise, it would not be possible to recognize dreams and reality as such. From this, Augustine recognizes the clear possibility of truth, and the reality of falsehood. Third, Augustine often puzzles over the power of memory and its ability to conjure, by recollection, images greater than the human spirit is able to contain. For instance, the image of Carthage, a city far away, suddenly and effortlessly arises in the imagination. This shows, in Augustine's words, that the memory is a place that is no place, where images of memory and imagination do not take up a place to convey reality. In other words, images are immaterial and extend beyond space. Lastly, and this is his favourite analogy to explore the deceitful aspect of images, Augustine often considers how mirror images resemble the reality of their sources. This leads him to ponder, how is it possible to discern between an image and its source? After much intrigue, he concludes, the source of the image has life, movement and being, while the reflection does not. These analogies deal with the deceitful aspect of images and allow Augustine, in considering falsehood not in isolation but in relation to truth and reality, to focus on resemblance as the pivotal function of images and the core of identity. Therefore, the passage above reveals, second, that images are inescapable mechanisms to discover and articulate the inherent alterity of identity. Yet this is not yet fully evident. Although eventually the metaphor of mirror images becomes the metaphor par excellence to explore the human predicament, this passage restricts the definition of truth to sameness. An image is true, only when it resembles exactly what it is representing. The truth of identity is therefore perfect likeness or equality. Identity is void of difference. Conversely, the false is what is not self-same or an image that resembles what it represents but not perfectly so. By implication, Augustine treats difference (to a source) as synonymous with falsehood and, therefore, as contrary to identity. Augustine then provides his most accurate definition of falsehood: 'nothing remains which can justly be called false, save that which deigns to be what it is not, or, in general, that which tends to be and is not.'[8] Truth is that which is identical, whereas falsehood or privation of truth is difference. Thus, the similarity and imitation of images inevitably and always fall short of identity. There is no truth outside of identity, and the falsehood of difference emerges as an ephemeral promise of belonging. To belong is therefore to reject falsehood and to escape difference while preserving sameness at any cost.

These important early observations by Augustine are replete with insight, which he later formalizes by locating perception and image representation within an ontological spectrum of likeness and unlikeness in 391. Before discussing this formalization, however, a few important implications and clarifications are worth mentioning. First, what philosophers call epistemology bears on considerations of ontology. This means that Augustine is not shy to make conclusions about the fundamental nature of reality based on his reflections about sense perception. Thus, observing that difference is the cause of falsehood in sense perception leads Augustine to conclude that the truth of identity must also depend on self-sameness and the exclusion of falsehood. Augustine engages with reality as a single tapestry and not piecemeal. This is significant, second, because it allows Augustine to introduce a normative dimension to the discussion of identity and belonging. If identity requires excluding truth in perception, and in the fabric of reality, then this implies also a normative claim. That is, difference must be rejected for the sake of sameness. This view is of utmost consequence. On the one hand, identity must exclude difference because difference is evil. Operative here is the view of evil as privation, analogous to difference in identity as falsehood. Certainly, who would want to include evil in identity? On the other hand, and this is one of the greatest insights of Western thought, what is most false, and therefore most evil and ontologically perverse, has the most semblance to truth. In other words, the truth of identity, and by implication its goodness and ontological integrity, is ever under suspicion of imperfect equality. The false is most false when it is most like the true. Semblance, mimicry and dissimulation are all inherent to falsehood, and therefore, they are to be avoided. To do this, a crucial reference for determining likeness and unlikeness, and by implication falsehood and truth of identity, is required. However, identifying such point of reference is not an easy task, even when trying to discern oneself from an image in the mirror, let alone oneself from others. Although this verges on the inevitability of a practical commitment to scepticism, it need not be so. Augustine faces three options. First, to identify a criterion to evaluate semblance. Second, to give up the hope of ever finding such a criterion. Third, to integrate semblance in the ontological framework of image. He follows the third option by adopting a Platonic ontology of image. In a Platonic ontology of image, there is a spectrum of dissemblance, or semblance, between a source, and its reflection or image. The more an image resembles its source, the more truthful and less false it becomes. Conversely, the less an image resembles its source, the less truthful and the more false it becomes. This is significant, for it means that at any given moment, images are simultaneously unlike their source in certain respect, but also like their source in another respect. Resemblance is not definable in the absolute because it is a continuum of (un)likeness. A spectrum of (un)likeness introduces the possibility of thinking about the truth of identity in terms of dynamic degrees of increasing resemblance. It also introduces the process of attaining similarity, by moving away from difference, as the moral itinerary of human life. However, this leaves Augustine with a paradox that illustrates the problem of identity. On the one hand, human beings must continuously reject difference to perfect and preserve the truth of identity. On the other hand, in the absence of a point of reference, a source to measure the ideal of true or perfect identity, and at the other end of the spectrum what is most inhuman, human identity remains a never-ending process of undefined transformations. Human identity is at once refusing difference yet remains ever reduced to difference, as there is no end goal to attaining similarity. Identity, in the absence of a point of reference, is difference in search for unattainable sameness. It is a redundant illusion. This is the heart of the problem of identity. Difference is inescapable, yet how to integrate it in sameness seems an inherent contradiction of the human predicament. Augustine offers a compelling response to this problem in 391 when, after ordination, he plunges into the study of the letters of Paul and thereafter formalizes the ontology of image to articulate identity as a continuum of (un)likeness.

The spectrum of likeness

To formalize the ontology of image as a continuum of (un)likeness, Augustine reads Genesis in light of the letters of Paul. Consequently, he considers Jesus as the image of God and human beings as the reflection or resemblance of God's image in Christ. Thus, while human beings imperfectly resemble the perfect image of God who is Christ, the image of God remains an unattainable ideal. This exacerbates the problem of belonging since according to this scheme the divine resemblance of human beings is restricted to likeness due to sin. Until 412, Augustine believed that human sin destroys the image of God in humanity. In other words, human beings are not inherently deformed and in need of reformation, as would be the case if the image of God were simply deformed – a position Augustine adopts after 412. Rather, the little resemblance human beings can have is not inherent but only an imitation. In all their efforts to imitate Christ, human beings due to sin do not approach equality but only reveal their falsehood. Thus, Augustine continues to struggle with the problematic and inescapable place of difference in identity.

Augustine considers the image of God in light of images in his writings as early as 386. The point of departure is a passage in the creation story in the book of Genesis, which would become a pivotal point of fruitful reflection, and even important to his conversion. That Augustine wrestled with the problematic implications of this passage for human identity for the next fifty years clearly shows that he understood how much rested on considering the origin of humanity in God. The fundamental insight of Genesis that captivated Augustine is that the truth of humanity is not a brute fact of reality readily available for consideration. Rather, the truth of human identity is inherent in the revelation of scripture, particularly in the creation story of Gen. 1.26. On the sixth day of creation, the truth of humanity's identity is revealed in God's image: 'God said, "Let us make man in our image, after our likeness. [. . .] So God created man in his own image, in the image of God he created him; male and female he created them."'[9] This does not mean human beings are equivocally the image of God. The focus of this pivotal passage, considered in isolation, is resemblance; human beings somehow resemble God. Unsurprisingly, employing a Platonic ontology of image was from early on, Augustine's approach to appreciating the centrality of the difference and the likeness of an image to understand human identity. Indeed, the problem of belonging as the determination of identity vis-à-vis alterity in terms of images arises contemporaneously with the treatment of the image of God, as suggested in the parallel and contemporaneous consideration of images in general around 386,[10] and the first occurrence of Gen. 1.26.[11] What to make of human identity as having a likeness or resemblance to a divine source? Within the Platonic framework, this requires an image source that Augustine identifies with Jesus Christ by 391. Following Paul's letter to the Col. 1.15, Jesus is the 'visible image of the invisible God'. Before that, however, Gen. 1.26 suggests that the enigma of the human predicament lies not in equality but in difference. Human beings are not God. Yet, simultaneously, they are somehow like God. To make sense of difference, Augustine focuses on human origin. To explore likeness, he eventually introduces Christ as the end of human life. Everything between absolute difference and perfect likeness is a paradox of simultaneous likeness and unlikeness, which constitutes the indefinability of humanity *in via*. Human beings stretch between their origin and their end in what Augustine calls in the *Confessions* 'a land of unlikeness'.[12]

Difference arises from the mode of human creation. God creates out of nothing (*ex nihilo*), according to the Christian tradition. This concept of 'creation out of nothing' aims to accentuate the metaphysical distance between God and humanity. From the outset, therefore, difference is the condition for the possibility of human existence. The first defining characteristic of humanity is a negative determination, namely, that human beings are not God. Conversely, this condition ensures a transcendent divine origin. In Christian cosmogony, God creates humanity and maintains a transcendent difference according to the mode of creation out of nothing. On this point, Augustine departs from Plato. In Plato's *Timaeus*, creation consists in forming unformed matter, not about creating inexistent matter. Augustine interprets this process not as giving form to pre-existent matter, as is the case for Plato, but as creating even unformed matter. The explanation for this passage from inexistence to existence is, of course, nothingness. That humanity has its origin in nothing ensures a relation to a transcendent divine origin while emphasizing the difference between God and human beings. At the extreme end of unlikeness from God, who simply *is* for Augustine the *idipsum* or the self-same, human beings bear, as a zeal of their origin, a daunting and constitutive metaphysical nothingness.[13] Thus, in contrast to the absolute being of God, the nothingness of human existence implies a positive and a negative differentiator. On the one hand, human beings relate to God. On the other hand, human beings are infinitely unlike God – Augustine eventually comes to understand the importance of this relational emphasis in mapping out the structure of alterity after the Trinity of God. Augustine later notes in an astute play of prepositions that human beings have an origin in God based on *ex nihilo* creation – this is, the positive dimension to human existence – but remain deeply unlike God, since they are created *de nihilo* or of nothing – this is, the negative dimension.[14] In other words, human beings are torn between (not) being, and becoming, between the positive difference of *ex nihilo* that allows them to pass from being to becoming, and the negative difference of *de nihilo*, which leaves humanity to remain ever undefined. Matthew Drever articulates this well: 'the *de nihilo* origin of creation generates an irreducible mutability that precludes the self-referential nature of the mind from finding a final grounding within the autonomy of its own substance, and in this points ultimately to its grounding in the divine image and so to our orientation toward God rather than our origins *de nihilo*.'¹⁵ Accordingly, humanity is not self-referential and seeks rest for its ontological restlessness. Drever continues, 'This leads to a complicated dynamic between the stability of having a capacity as the image of the immutable God and the mutability of having our origin *de nihilo*.'¹⁶ The *de nihilo* and *ex nihilo* origin of humanity captures the existential fissure with which Augustine contends in the journey towards conversion and leading up to his baptism. In this dyadic ambivalence, the mystery of human existence unfolds as this 'life that dies, this death that lives'.¹⁷ In bearing some likeness to God, and without being of God, in virtue of creation *ex/de nihilo*, humanity seems reduced to absolute metaphysical difference, both negative and positive. For instance, years later, anticipating the Cartesian 'I think therefore I am' (*cogito ergo sum*), Augustine elegantly situates the falsehood of difference as the ground of human existence in *City of God*, composed after 412. He writes, 'if I am mistaken, I am.'¹⁸ In this citation, Augustine articulates the nothingness of difference in an epistemological formulation where difference is the manifestation of the deepest truth about humanity.

Although some have attempted to make of difference the indefinable descriptive definition of human difference, Augustine pries further into the depths of the human mystery. This time, he turns to the reverse side of the coin of similitude, away from dissemblance and into the question of likeness. The pressing question at this point is this: Is likeness possible at all? How to reconcile the *ex/de nihilo* account of creation with the Platonic account of image? What, in other words, is the positive human likeness to God, if any? The answer to this question goes in hand with the journey of Augustine's conversion and the discovery of the incarnational, where Christ the Word of God shares 'in the garments of our flesh'.¹⁹ Namely, an intermediate between God and humanity is required, 'the Mediator between God and human beings, the human being Christ Jesus'.²⁰ Jesus, considered as 'the visible image of the invisible God'²¹ in Paul's letter to the Colossians, would serve a double function in Augustine's engagement with articulating positively the truth of human identity. On the one hand, Jesus considered as the perfect image of God functions to reveal the humanity of humanity. The incarnation was therefore the requirement for the positive manifestation of human identity. This would mean that difference and sameness within the Platonic framework of identity are somehow complete. However, this does not completely overcome the problem of identity. On the contrary, it shifts the attention to what becomes the programmatic itinerary of Augustine's engagement with the problem of belonging: namely, first, realizing that the dynamism of alterity is constitutive of human identity and, second, reconsidering and reconceptualizing human identity not as a project to obtain sameness at the expense of difference but as a challenge to articulate identity in terms of alterity. Without the incarnation, the chasm of difference between God and humanity is too vast to overcome.

Upon becoming a priest in 391, Augustine turned to the study of the letters of Paul. This, together with a series of questions penned by his friends on various topics, occasioned the completion of the Platonic spectrum of image to construe the identity of humanity. In the far end of unlikeness was the creative act of God from nothingness that grounds ontological difference. The as-of-yet incomplete other end of likeness, perfect likeness to God, which is what offered the possibility of likeness whatsoever, was found in Paul. In a passage of Colossians, Paul identifies Jesus as 'the visible image of the invisible God'.[22] Reading Gen. 1.26 in light of this passage and within the spectrum of Platonic ontology of image, the question becomes, how does Christ as the perfect image of God, and by implication as God, relate to humanity made in the likeness of God? Augustine provides the answers in an important passage: 'Image and equality and likeness must be differentiated, because where there is an image there is necessarily a likeness but not necessarily equality; where there is equality there is necessarily a likeness but not necessarily an image; where there is a likeness there is not necessarily an image and not necessarily equality.'[23] The analysis in this passage brings together a number of key elements to the discussion of the truth of human identity understood in terms of image. These are the notions of image, likeness and equality. These terms, with obvious ontological import, relate in terms of what they necessarily imply or not. Augustine explains them in terms of relation. This is important because relation eventually becomes a central question in thinking about the Trinity and about the alterity of identity. The first is a relation of image. All images necessarily imply a likeness. To be an image, is to be an image of something. Therefore, to the extent that the something in question is represented or manifested, a likeness of an image, no matter how accurate or not, always bears a likeness of its source. If there is no likeness to a source, then logically there is no image. This brings

Augustine to the second relation. An image is always a likeness of a source. If the image does not resemble the source, then it is not an image. Conversely, however, likeness allows for various degrees of resemblance. Therefore, not all likeness implies perfect likeness. Some images may be more like their source than others may. The second is a relation of equality. Not all things equal are necessarily images of each other. The classic example Augustine uses is that of eggs. Two eggs bear likeness to each other, but they are not for this reason alone images of one another. However, equal things always bear a perfect likeness. For instance, an egg in front of a mirror is an equal image of its source. In this case, the likeness is perfect because the source and the image are equal. Thus, equality always implies likeness. The third is a relation of likeness. Likeness does not necessarily imply either an image or an equality. For instance, a piece of white cotton is like a white egg in so far as both have the same colour, but it is neither the image of the egg nor an egg. Thus, cotton and an egg are like each other, but they are neither images of each other or equal to each other. What does Augustine make of this analysis of image, equality and likeness? In 391, Christ alone is the image of God. This means Christ has perfect likeness to God and Christ is therefore equal to God. Accordingly, Christ is an image, a likeness and an equal of God. Christ is God. Human beings, however, are not the image of God. In fact, Augustine believes that this image mentioned in Gen. 1.26 was lost due to sin. Not until 412 does Augustine reconsider this position. In the meantime, the notion of likeness is the conceptual tool that best captures the human condition. Human beings are somehow like God, as revealed in the perfect image who is Christ, but neither equal nor the image of God. This situation of positive likeness or semblance is important to understanding human identity in terms of the truth of images. Whereas in considering creation the emphasis rested on a difference, positive and negative, now in considering the incarnation a positive likeness is possible because the image of God is the visible point of reference in the incarnation of the Word. God is therefore at both ends of the spectrum of likeness in Christ and unlikeness in God's creative act. Accordingly, human beings are at once unlike God and like God. This captures the metaphysical ambivalence of the human condition, which requires integrating difference and sameness, dynamically and simultaneously, by oscillating between existence and nothingness. This also presents the imitation of Christ, the *sequela Christi*, as the sure moral itinerary to escape the nothingness of finitude. Seeking likeness to God in Christ is the response to resisting the nothingness of human life. The concepts of the truth of image and the falsehood of image are henceforth different sides of the same coin. To understand falsehood as a privation does not mean understanding it merely as the antipode of truth, but as a metaphysical condition for the possibility thereof. As such, falsehood and semblance of truth are paradoxical and inescapable requirement of identity. At this point, Augustine is preoccupied with the challenging task of determining what exactly is the human (un)likeness in relation to Christ according to two conditions. First, human beings cannot be the image of God, for this would make gods of human beings. Second, in being like Christ, human beings are also somehow divine; otherwise, there is no likeness to God. This is no easy task and remains, in a sense, unresolved by this framework discovered in 391.

Identifying the likeness of humanity to God was a long journey for Augustine. The Manichean derision of the body proved to be an obstacle for Augustine when thinking about the human likeness in the image of God, for this would seem to imply that God is material. Just as the Manichean interpretation of the material divine image initially kept Augustine away from the Catholic faith, Ambrose's spiritual interpretation proved to be crucial for his return. The predominant view in Augustine's milieu was that God is corporeal. This was the view of Augustine's North African predecessor Tertullian, for instance. To say that human beings were like God conversely implied that God is like humans. This resulted in a problem of anthropomorphism – projecting into God human characteristics. The literal interpretation of Genesis, believed Augustine before his conversion, demanded this kind of interpretation and, with the Manicheans, ridiculed the belief in the image of God as an unsophisticated position. With his encounter with Ambrose and the Platonists in Milan came a decisive moment in the discovery of an alternative way of reading the story of Genesis through a spiritual lens. Augustine writes:

> And I had not yet learned that God is a spirit, that he has no parts spread out with length and breadth, that he has no bulk – for what has bulk has parts smaller than the whole, and if it is infinite, it is smaller in any determinate region of space than it is in its infinity, and so it does not exist as a whole everywhere, as a

spirit does, as God does. And I was utterly ignorant of what there is in us by which we are, and are rightly said in Scripture to be, in the image of God.[24]

The implication of this insight is that since God is not corporeal but spirit, so too are the traces of divinity in human spirit. Ambrose applied this spiritual reading to grasp Gen. 1.26. Ambrose's homilies on creation influenced Augustine on this matter. This put to rest the Manichean ridicule of Gen. 1.26. Augustine writes of his reaction to listening to Ambrose speak: 'And as I opened my heart to acknowledge how beautifully he spoke, I was likewise struck by how truly he spoke, though this happened only gradually.'[25] He continues, 'I was delighted to hear Ambrose in his popular sermons often commending this passage, most insistently, as a rule to be followed: "The letter kills, but the spirit gives life." When the Old Testament scriptures taken literally seemed to teach perversity.'[26] From Ambrose's preaching, Augustine learnt that 'the flesh therefore, cannot be made in the image of God'.[27] Since what is not flesh is spirit in the Platonic dualistic world view, this means the only contender left to resemble God is the spiritual aspect of human beings, namely the soul. Ambrose concludes: 'our soul, therefore, is made to the image of God. In this is man's entire essence.'[28] Augustine adopts Ambrose's teachings and rejects a material reading of the divine image, as can be seen, when he writes in *Confessions*: 'I discovered that your spiritual children, those who through grace have been reborn from our mother, the catholic Church, did not understand the claim that human beings were created in the image of God to mean that you are bounded within the shape of a human body – that was not what they believed, not how they thought of you.'[29] Augustine thus found belonging in the Catholic faith by asserting Ambrose's spiritual reading that the truth of humanity is in God's image. The soul, therefore, is the likeness of humanity to God. The soul is the divine spark in human beings. It is not the image of God but resembles the invisible aspect of Christ who alone is the perfect and visible image of God. Namely, the divinity of the incarnation. What about the soul is like God, who is fundamentally spirit? Its immortality, its indeterminacy, its immutability. This completes the spectrum of dissemblance. The identity of human beings resembling the image of God in spirit suspends the soul between the nothingness of its origin *de/ex nihilo* and its perfect manifestation in Christ.

Accordingly, difference and sameness appear integrated into the identity of what it means to be human. The question is, at what cost?

Considering how integrating difference and sameness in identity comes at the expense of materiality, the body, and all that follows thereof, leads to reconsider the centrality of the paradoxes of alterity within human identity. Wagering the death of the body for the life of the spirit initially proved to be useful for Augustine in his effort to address certain difficulties, such as the notion that there is a trace of divinity in all of humanity. This trace was thus reduced to a spiritual vestige of God in humanity. However, this ultimately exacerbated the problem of belonging for Augustine, as he would later find while wrestling with the implications of his newly adopted position. That Augustine was dissatisfied with simply spiritualizing and internalizing the divine image is evidenced by the fact that he continued to articulate a literal interpretation of Gen. 1.26, yet left the commentaries of Genesis incomplete precisely at this point.[30] He continued wrestling to find a literal meaning of the human likeness to God throughout his life but to no avail. Augustine's commentary would not produce a literal rendering. An alternative strategy to come to grips with the place of alterity in identity was to clarify what it was about the soul that resembled God. Augustine, for example, at one point, insists on reading 1 Cor. 11.7 in a way that locates the divine image in the rational and incorporeal mind.[31] With this, Augustine attempts to escape the problem of corporeal individuation. In so doing, Augustine does not restrict the incorporeal divine image to either only men or women but, rather, extends it to all of humanity. The result is that image of God is asexual because it is incorporeal. Interestingly, confronted with the fact of human sexual difference, an implication of corporeality for Augustine, leads him, for the first time, to how the complementarity of difference in a sense constitutes a wholesome identity in the likeness of the image of God. This growingly positive attitude towards alterity, however, does not ease the paradoxical contraposition which he identifies between identity and difference and which he still finds difficult to integrate into the architecture of belonging. Augustine maintains that women are divine images not as women but as human beings irrespective of their individual sexuality and through their complementarity in difference. Furthermore, metaphorically speaking, Augustine maintains that man alone reflects the active aspect of the divine image, while woman represents the passive part of the intellect. The complementarity of the sexes reveals the image of God only by way of analogy irrespective of the body. Hence, again at the expense of the body and consequently by excluding sexual difference, Augustine twice insists in *On the Trinity* that the image of God is 'where there is no sex'.[32] The tension at the heart of the problem of alterity is incipient in the metaphorical reservation of the divine image to man. Echoing his commentaries on Genesis, Augustine excludes woman from the image of God in *On the Trinity*, thereby reserving the metaphorical approximation to the divine image only to men. The thrust of the problem here is not primarily one of gender, as some commentators have argued, but alterity and identity. Humanity imagined as a disincarnate and asexual abstraction was Augustine's only way to consider the likeness of the spiritual image of God.[33] The implication in the resulting complementarity in difference is that women are subjected to men.[34] The inherent tensions of Augustine's sweeping conclusion whereby male and female are equal in terms of spiritual complementarity, but unequal in practice, is epitomized in a later text where Augustine calls woman 'the inferior sex'.[35] Yet, at around the same time he writes elsewhere that women have the 'the stronger affect'.[36] Clearly, the complex tension between difference and identity endured for many years without an obvious resolution. Although Augustine's acceptance of the divine image initially relied upon his spiritual engagement with the question of the truth of humanity, he ultimately regarded foregoing corporeality as too high of a price to pay, for it raised far more questions than it provided answers. Complimentary is a first attempt not to reject but, rather, to engage with alterity. Waged at the price of the body, however, complementarity foregoes sexual individuation and reduces falsehood to affirmation. Thus, in his early engagement with the problem of belonging, Augustine integrates difference into the image of God by rejecting the notion of corporeal alterity. Augustine gradually developed sophisticated ways to deal with the alterity of the body and its relation to the soul and, most importantly, how these together resembled God. Thus, while the formalization of the ontology of image articulated in 391 offers a first step to engage with alterity, defining its place in human identity remains unresolved. It is unresolved to the extent that this framework fails to capture the ongoing place of alterity in defining human existence. Alterity, Augustine came to understand, is not to be discarded but integrated into the human constitution. This framework of the ontology of image reveals the difficulty with seeking the divinity of humanity in the humanity of Christ's divinity in terms of likeness only and in terms of a purely monadic God reminiscent of the Platonic One and the *idipsum* of Exodus. Pure unity cannot be the reference point for humanity's alterity, for this implies alterity must ultimately resolve in sameness. However, Augustine later realized that this is impossible because the paradoxes of alterity are part of what it means to be human.

The limits of dyadic alterity

With time, Augustine realizes that alterity is not simply undone by finding identity in sameness because the interplay of sameness and difference is inherent to the constitution of human existence. He experienced the existential alterity of restlessness, as evidenced in his opening of *Confessions*, 'Restless are we until our hearts find rest in you.'[37] The 'you' here is a condition for rest, for unity, for identity. This 'you', as of yet, is monadic; however, it is God modelled after the Platonic self-same and diffusing One. Initially, this model was expedient, as it resonated with the manifestation of God's name to Moses in the burning bush as the *idipsum* or the self-same: 'God said to Moses, "I am who I am." And he said, "Say this to the people of Israel: 'I am has sent me to you.'"'[38] Alternatively, the translation may read, 'I will be what I will be.' In this tautological manifestation of God, by God, to Moses, the perfect divine identity, the model and ground of all identities, aligns well with the incomprehensible and undivided unity of the Platonic One, where there is no difference, no time, no change, only immovable eternity. All identity, therefore, must imitate the self-same unity of God. This poses a problem, however. If God is One, by implication, the antidote to the infirmity of interior alterity from whence humanity arises as a question unto itself, consists in the obliteration of difference. However, is this possible without also destroying what it means to be human? Upon considering the full weight of the post-Nicaean creed, and specifically, the belief in a God who is one, yet somehow also triune, it was only a matter of time before Augustine fully understood the structure of human alterity in terms of the triadic image of God. Dyadic alterity, in other words, within a spectrum of likeness, required the addition of 'a third' in relation. In the model of the Trinitarian structure, which Augustine explores extensively in *On the Trinity*, God is a single deity, and a triad of ontological difference, captured by the complex term 'person' (*persona*). Then alone, following the triadic structure of God, alterity constitutes identity and safeguards difference. The move towards a triune model was a choice for difference in identity over unity at the expense of difference, as was the case with the monadic One of Plato. This marked, conversely, a move away from the consideration of human identity as self-same unity. The likeness of humanity to God turned into a Trinitarian vestige, a triadic trace of God in the human soul. To be self-same, even in the divine structure, was to discover difference as a condition for sameness. Ironically, therefore, the Platonic ontology of image accentuated for Augustine the need to integrate the paradoxes of alterity within identity and in so doing to move away from Platonic unity as the beginning and end of all things. To be precise, there is unity, yes, even in the Trinity, but this unity does not discard difference but depends on its interplay. Trinitarian unity is a novel understanding of identity, based on a properly Christian concept of God, where difference and sameness interact to form a whole where alterity primes. This view would come only over time by realizing why the unity of the One could not capture the inherent alterity of human identity. As noted before, Augustine gradually appreciated the place of alterity in identity by following the powerful Platonic ontology of image. By 391, as noted earlier, Augustine had constructed a compelling framework to make sense of human identity in terms of image. At one end of the spectrum was humanity's origin in God *ex/de nihilo* and at the other end of the spectrum was Jesus Christ, the Son of God, and the visible image of the invisible God, in the words of Paul. The spectrum located human beings within the extremes of unlikeness to God in the *nihil* or nothingness, and perfect likeness of God, namely the equality with God, in Christ. Accordingly, the determining characteristic of the human condition resulted in a dynamic ambivalence, oscillating simultaneously between the likeness of God and the unlikeness of God. Although this implied foregoing material difference, the complex spectrum offered a compelling initial model to integrate the alterity of sameness and difference in human identity as different sides of the same coin.

The dynamism of alterity is operative in how Augustine ultimately deals with the identity of humanity's likeness to God's image as a wholesome reality. This notion of likeness suspended human beings between absolute being (God) and the absence thereof (evil) or the *privatio boni*,[39] and therefore oriented identity within the alterity of good and evil (ontology), being and non-being (metaphysics), truth and falsehood (epistemology), memory and forgetfulness (psychology), presence and absence (semiotics), time and eternity (temporality). Operative in the foreground is a commitment to the Platonic view of the good as 'emanating', not temporally, but ontologically, or as self-diffusing (*bonum est diffusivum sui*), and of evil, by implication, not as the effect of good but as the privation of goodness (*privatio boni*). Importantly, the Platonic approach avoided the dualism of the Manicheans. This was, in fact, the first paradox of alterity, which Augustine first encountered. With the Manicheans, Augustine believed evil and good were opposing real entities. Augustine writes, 'For it was not merely that I did not know that evil was not a substance: I actually thought it was a bodily substance; I did not even know how to think about mind except as a fine body that was somehow diffused throughout space.'[40] Eventually, Augustine comes to appreciate, with the Platonists, that evil is not a substance, 'I had no idea what I was saying. I did not know, I had not learned, that evil is not a substance, or that our own mind is not the supreme and unchangeable good.'[41] Thus, goodness defines evil. Evil is not goodness but the absence of the good. This is difficult to understand. If the good is self-diffusive, in what place – that is no place – does the good not diffuse in such a way that there is privation or evil? A metaphor may be useful to understand this problem. For Augustine, goodness is the metaphysical condition for the possibility of evil. Consider a tapestry or a painting. The darkness represents the *nihil* that is not God. The less light there is, the darker the colours become. Yet, it is not possible to understand what the dark shades are without the light, and even though the absence of light is not light, the positive name of darkness is used to denote it. This does not mean, however, that by naming it, it also necessarily exists as light. Ultimately, in the world, in the spectrum of (un)likeness that Augustine uses to articulate human identity, these two, goodness and its absence (evil), always coexist dynamically. This is the basis for Augustine later stating in *City of God* that the heavenly and the earthly cities coexist. It is also the basis for the belief, against the Donatists, that the church is a mixed church with good and bad people. This is the same reasoning applied to account for being and non-being in *creatio ex/de nihilo*. All that exists comes from God and, in this sense, has a positive existence. However, to say that God creates from nothing and that human beings are of nothing does not mean the *nihil* has a positive metaphysical status. Rather, the *nihil* is an absolute conceptual absence. It is not antipode of God as absolute negative existence, but the ultimate absence of being, in the utmost extreme of the spectrum of unlikeness to God, where there simply is no existence. The concept of *nihil* in a sense has a mediation role to differentiate God from creation. This proves all the more powerful a consideration to think about the weight of nothingness against which human beings unceasingly contend. For the same reason, Augustine describes early on in his dialogues that falsehood is that which most resembles what is true. Falsehood does not have a positive existence. The characteristic of falsehood is mimicry unto its object of resemblance, while remaining ever different. Eventually, the same mechanism surfaces to answer how it is possible that forgetfulness can be the content of memory. Augustine notes that 'it is I who remember, I the mind . . . What is nearer to me than I myself?'[42] He insists 'that I have remembered forgetfulness itself, whereby what I remember is destroyed.'[43] This is possible because there is no content to forgetfulness; it is not a memory as such. Forgetfulness is a vestige of the memory it once was. This absence of memory triggers recollection. Since identity depends on memory and a unified narrative of human life, in this identity emerges as the presence of an absence (difference) and absence of a presence (sameness). This analysis of memory unfolds a central aspect of Augustinian communication or semiotics, whereby absence is a trace of presence. The sign implies the absence of the signified, but in signifying, the sign in a sense makes presence what is being signified. Signs convey something other than themselves. This means an identity is possible in the midst of an absence, precisely because of the paradoxes of alterity. Augustine therefore does not forego identity at the expense of its paradoxes. Rather, being fond of paradox and rhetorical eloquence, he embarked upon integrating paradoxes within the constitution of identity. What emerges is a divided interiority and the need for God to integrate it. These paradoxes of alterity are the constitutive restlessness of human existence. That is why the human heart finds only rest in divine unity, 'our heart is restless until it comes to rest in you.'[44] The disquietude of the human spirit is that it longs to find rest in God because, on its own, the soul is incomplete. For this reason, human beings are a question unto themselves. As Augustine puts it when addressing God, 'But you were more deeply within me than the innermost part of my being, higher than what was highest in me.'[45] Alterity runs deep within the constitution of human existence and emerges as the condition for self-knowledge where he states, 'O you who know me: let me know you; let me know even as I am known.'[46] Thus, being known is the condition to know oneself. To be is to be perceived, as Augustine notes. The possibility of human life, in other words, depends on alterity. 'Am I not myself when I am asleep, O Lord my God? Yet there is such a difference between myself and myself in that moment in which I pass from wakefulness to sleep or return from sleep to wakefulness!'[47] The mystery of human alterity escapes understanding. He continues, 'I cannot contain everything that I am [. . .] People go forth to wonder at the heights of mountains, the vast waves of the sea, waterfalls of immense breadth, the expanse of the ocean, the courses of the stars – but they pay no heed to themselves.'[48] The complexity of interiority reveals alterity as its possibility: 'But you were more deeply within me than the innermost part of my being, higher than what was highest in me.'[49]

That alterity is constitutive of human identity and that likeness is its most accurate mode of representation is due to time. As the likeness of God, who is eternal, human beings are the moving image of eternity. Time is the paradigmatic expression of human likeness and therefore of difference. In time lies the mystery of humanity's constitution of alterity. According to Plato, in his work on cosmogony, the *Timaeus*, 'time is a moving image of eternity'. If God is eternity, this means time is a moving likeness of God. Furthermore, if human beings are the likeness of God, this means human beings are, at least partly, the moving likeness of eternity. In other words, the likeness of humanity to God captured in the relation of time to eternity: human beings are time. This temporal constitution accounts for the ontological necessity of the paradoxes of difference in human identity and the ongoing challenge to harmonize the restlessness of life. This is expedient, for then human beings are the likeness of eternity, and in their motion betray their deeply dynamic and passing constitution. Perhaps this is the single best reason as to why human beings are a paradox of alterity: human beings are time, passing away, 'this life that dies, this death that lives'.[50] Time as the likeness of eternity reveals life as a process of being and becoming, and, conversely, being and unbecoming. Humans are beings of time. The passing of human life conceals the great mystery of the alterity of human constitution, constantly in the process of becoming what it is to be and passing into what has been. In contrast to the becoming of human temporality,

Plotinus describes eternity in *Enneads* as 'something which abides in the same in itself and does not change at all but is always in the present, because nothing of it has passed away, nor again will anything of it come into being, but that which it is, it is'.[51] Unceasing movement of time is what differentiates it from the unending rest of eternity. The *idipsum* of God is due to stability whereas the restless squandering of human life in the river of time is inevitable due to time. Better yet, due to being on time and of time. Augustine describes time, and therefore, being in time, as 'the tendency not to be'.[52] This does not mean life is a positive unbecoming unto death. Rather, for Augustine, this means life as mutability is the absence of the unity of God's stability as the *idipsum*. To find stability is nothing short of becoming eternal. A century later, Boethius bridges Augustine's adoption of Plotinus by defining eternity as 'the perfect possession all at once of unending life'.[53] Becoming one implies rest, a new-grounded substance, and alterity is the truth of the human condition immersed in the river of time. Augustine initially engages with this realization in terms of likeness and unlikeness due to considering God in terms of the unity of oneness and the absence of difference. However, upon reconsideration, and in an attempt to grasp the paradox of alterity constitutive of human identity, Augustine realizes human alterity is also a vestige of the divine Trinitarian alterity. The task towards recovering the structure of identity is to model human life according to the unity in difference of the Trinity. This becomes the image of God in humanity and the blueprint of identity as a longing to be, or be-longing in likeness. Thus, by discovering the alterity of identity, ironically through the conflation of the divinely manifested *idipsum* to the Platonic One, Augustine reconsiders the likeness of humanity to God in two important respects. On the one hand, likeness is no longer oriented towards a resolution in the imitation of unity. Rather, likeness obtains a more defined status, particularly in its expression of Trinitarian alterity. Accordingly, human identity resembles God in the interplay of alterity and the preservation difference in unity. On the other hand, this allows Augustine to reconsider by 412 that human beings are not only a likeness but also an image of God. The discovery of alterity leads Augustine to understand, from above (God) and from below (humanity), that the first is foremost triune, and by implication that the second is more divine in its alterity than Augustine was ready to concede following a Plotinian vision of the One. In other words, the discovery of alterity in the problem of identity brings Augustine closer to the notion that human beings do not just resemble God but are also disfigured images of God. Upon reflection, Augustine realizes by 412, human beings have likeness to God because they are images of God. This paves the way to articulate the structure of alterity as the triadic image of God, albeit an imperfect or disfigured image of God. Discovering alterity allowed Augustine to understand that a reflection is not only the likeness but also the deformed distortion of an image. Thus, seeing through a glass, at first implied for Augustine reflecting an effaced image of God. So disfigured was the reflection that Augustine concluded that the mirror image is no image at all but only a likeness. However, the more Augustine understood this likeness in the interplay of alterity, the more he discovered this divine image was not effaced but defaced. Humanity is a deformed image of God, not an image destroyed. Overcoming the problem of identity meant, therefore, reforming this image and perfecting it into the likeness of the divine triadic alterity as the most authentic manifestation of human life. Henceforth, Augustine reconsiders the integral di-stance of humanity in the interplay of sameness and difference in light of the Trinity.

Conclusion

To capture the enigma of human life as a question unto itself, Augustine explores identity in terms of image. This is the case for three reasons. First, images have a property of likeness and likeness implies unlikeness. Therefore, as the likeness of a divine image, human beings bear a constitutive and irreducible sameness and difference. Second, since likeness is not an absolute category, not yet at least, Augustine instinctively locates the human condition within an ontological spectrum of image. Likeness is a relation. It is therefore a likeness of something. Augustine locates likeness between two poles of resemblance. At one extreme is the perfect divine *idipsum* or self-same. This is the One of Plotinus, whom Augustine expediently conflates with God. At the other extreme are inexistence or nothingness (*nihil*) and privation. Human beings stand between these extremes as likenesses in dynamic becoming, constantly wagering a flimsy posture of simultaneous difference and sameness. Finally, by implication, human beings are always bound to remain semblances of an image. Accordingly, it is simply impossible to reduce likeness to unified sameness or unlikeness to pure difference. Any attempts to the contrary are bound to fail. In other words, the paradox of alterity is the fundamental composition of human existence.

This has important implications when considering the problem of belonging and the effect of distance on the possibility of belonging during confinement. Belonging at a distance is not only possible but rather a necessary integral component of human authenticity. While intuitively most people believe presence is a requirement for belonging, considered as a metaphor for difference, belonging in confinement suddenly reveals the truth of human existence. That is, the paradox of alterity characterizes human life as a question unto itself. The difference of distance is not an obstacle to belonging. Rather, the problem of belonging, of longing to be and of being in longing is the mode of human becoming as a 'this life that dies, this death that lives'.[54] This is because, as Augustine slowly realized, alterity is part of identity. In longing, difference emerges not as an obstacle to overcome but as a constitutive dynamism of human belonging. From this vantage point, distancing occasions a malaise because distancing is a reminder of the interior fragmentation and constitutive alterity of identity. Therefore, the reaction in times of pandemic and isolation has been to conflate difference with distance and to conclude that belonging at a distance is consequently not possible, and indeed an impossible feat, a contradiction in terms. Belonging is incomplete, many believe, unless somehow distance turns into presence. According to this sentiment, belonging is not possible without presence. Yet upon recognizing that difference is part of identity, presence is no longer a requirement for belonging. On the contrary, during the confinement, distance has revealed the uneasy and fragmented truth of belonging and human identity. By implication, belonging opens as a possibility in the midst of distance and absence. According to this analysis, conflating presence with belonging and absence with distance (and therefore incomplete or unattainable belonging) reveals one of two attitudes. First, distance is an unwanted difference. Second, conversely, presence is sameness achieved. Either case oversees alterity. Beyond the longing to *be*, the distance of confinement reveals the dynamics of human belonging as alterity, where belonging is about *longing* to be. To capture the problem of identity, Augustine avoids totalizing difference in the homogeneity of sameness and, simultaneously, evades the heterogeneity of radical difference. Instead, he preserves the two in a dynamism of becoming. Di-stance is therefore the double stance of the human predicament between being (sameness) and longing (difference), comprising be-longing. Di-stance is be-longing. Thus, the difference of distance reveals that human identity is a paradox of alterity. Now the question arises, what is the structure of the paradox of alterity? Without destroying the interplay of difference and sameness in identity, is it possible to capture the blueprint of belonging in a structure of alterity? Augustine answers these questions in reconsidering humanity in terms of divine alterity, no longer only as self-same unity but as a life of Trinity. Therein, the relation of alterity is not simply accidental but also substantial.

2

The structure of belonging

The possibility of belonging at a distance depends on recognizing the dynamism of alterity constitutive of human identity. However, what exactly is the structure of this dynamism? Failure to recognize the dynamism of alterity is a failure to belong at a distance. Therefore, the answer to this question is the next step in determining what it means to belong in the church during times of pandemic and isolation. Accordingly, this chapter argues that alterity is the structure of identity, from whence belonging emerges irrespective of social distance and physical absence. In revealing the constitution of human identity, the difference of distance offers the conditions to discover the integral structure of alterity. Augustine discovers the alterity of the human constitution as triadic based on considering God as not simply One but also, and simultaneously, as somehow Triune. Reconsidering God as triadic urges Augustine to understand the structure of belonging. In light of God's creation, human beings bear a vestige of God's Trinity. Furthermore, since the category of relation is essential to integrate divine oneness and Threeness, by implication the divine triadic vestige in humanity is also relation. Finally, since the incarnation reveals the relational dimension of the God's Trinity, the body is also a sign of God and therefore integral to the structure of alterity. To conclude, the structure of alterity is triadic, after the Triune God, and is revealed as relation and manifested in Christ. The church is Augustine's paradigm of belonging, where triadic dynamism, construed as incarnational relation, provides a blueprint to chart the structure of belonging.

Triadic dynamism

Having discovered the inherent alterity of belonging, Augustine integrates it as the structure of human identity. This is possible by relying on an ontology of image, on the one hand, and by replacing, or at least adapting, the Plotinian self-same One for the Triune God of Christianity on the other. The doctrine of the Trinity emerged progressively in early Christianity. It affirms the monotheistic principle of God, while maintaining, in addition, that God is also a triad, inherently a Trinity. Early proponents of this doctrine identified scriptural passages for its support, such as the commissioning of Christ to make disciples of all nations in the name of 'the Father, the Son and the Spirit'. This commissioning implied something of a divine Threeness. How to reconcile the triadic unity of God while fulfilling the requirement of monotheism and Trinity was far from obvious. Various formulas emerged over time to explain the mystery of the simultaneous divine unity in the triad of Father, Son and Spirit. At play in this formulation is, naturally, difference and sameness and the undivided unity of alterity. At play, however, is no longer the Plotinian dyadic alterity but a triadic dynamism. Theologians and philosophers wrestled with the problem of maintaining the distinction of Father, Son and Spirit while safeguarding their unblemished unity as one God. To do this, it was necessary to develop and apply sophisticated conceptual categories. After all, what to name the three – Father, Son and Spirit – and how to convey their undivided unity without compromising their threefold difference? Two important historical moments formalized this complex task. The first moment safeguarded the preservation of unity. In the year 325, a gathering called the Council of Nicaea introduced the Greek term ὁμοούσιον or *homoousion* to describe the relationship of the divine triad. As the compound word implies, the terms of the triad have a same being, or *homos* meaning same and *ousia*, translated as being or substance. The Father, Son and Spirit are therefore of the same being or substance. The term 'substance' is complex and, for a number of reasons, in revisiting Aristotle, Augustine later expresses in *On the Trinity* his preference for the term essence, rather than substance, to translate the original Greek *ousia*. For now, of importance is that the concept of 'same substance' captures the metaphysical unity of Father, Son and Spirit in the divine Trinity. During his lifetime, Augustine championed the aftermath of Nicaea's *homoousion*. The second moment was a triumph in the preservation of difference. The corresponding concept to articulate and formalize difference emerged in the Council of Constantinople in 381. This was the concept of *hypostasis* (ὑπόστα σις). In Latin, this Greek word was translated as *persona*, meaning person. Thus, the triadic difference is captured by the distinction of persons. The Father is a person, the Son is a different person from the Father and the Spirit a third person still, different from both the Father and the Son. The resulting articulation of the dogma of the Trinity by the early fifth century in mainstream Christianity is as follows. The Trinity of God consists of three distinct persons sharing a single substance. Augustine thus received this framework of Trinitarian alterity from the Christian milieu. Consequently, he quickly replaced the self-same One of Plotinus, as the source and end of the human likeness to God, for the divine Trinity. This implied the dyadic sameness/difference of likeness, which proved complicated for Augustine as has been discussed, could now be easily adapted into a framework of triadic alterity.

Accordingly, *On the Trinity* marks an important development in Augustine's thought. There, Augustine begins to integrate internal alterity into the truth of human beings. In so doing, he eventually reconstitutes the structure of belonging, the locus for which becomes the community of the church. The project of *On the Trinity* is to locate the vestiges of God's imprint in humanity. This imprint resembles God's triadic alterity. Therefore, Augustine seeks analogies for the Trinity of God, first in human experience and then in the mind. The passage of Genesis citing 'let us' is an indication that God creates as Trinity and accordingly, any likeness that humanity bears to God must also be Trinitarian. In humanity's origin, according to Genesis, God acts as Triune. Thus, Augustine notes:

> there is a preferable choice of meaning in these divine words, of why we should understand that it was said in the plural and not in the singular, 'Let us make man to our image and likeness'; it is that man was made to the image, not of the Father alone or of the Son alone or of the Holy Spirit alone, but of the Trinity itself.[1]

Thereafter, Augustine qualifies this plurality:

> This Trinity is a triad in such a way as to be one God, is one God in such a way as to be a triad. After all he did not say, as though speaking to the Son, Let us make man to your image – or to my

image – but he said in the plural, to our image and likeness; and who would dare to exclude the Holy Spirit from this plurality?²

Imprinted in the creation by a Triune God is the possibility to perceive the structure of humanity. In this, difference and sameness harmonize in the constitution of human existence. This implies from creation, that human beings are capable of the Triune God. Augustine notes: 'And you teach them – for now they have the capacity – to see the Trinity in Unity and the Unity in Trinity.'³ Creation instils the triadic structure of humanity and the capacity to recognize it. Augustine continues, 'And that is why an expression in the plural, "Let us make human beings," is nonetheless followed by an expression in the singular, "and God made human beings"; and the plural "according to our image" is followed by the singular "in the image of God."'⁴ A unidimensional immaterial soul proves henceforth unsatisfactory. The soul, like God, must be Trinitarian. Yet still operating within an ontology of (un)likeness, the more an analogy resembles God, the more it also proves unlike God. The search for a Trinitarian image in the soul is a project, therefore, of realizing the infinite distance between God and humanity. When all analogies to speak of God fail, only the dynamism of alterity remains. In *On the Trinity*, Augustine construes the image of God as an image of the Trinity, and alterity thus surfaces as the deepest vestige of God's hallmark in humanity. Upon exploring memory's contents in search for God, Augustine comes to the realization: 'there is a certain image of the Trinity: the mind itself, its knowledge, which is its offspring, and love as a third; these three are one and one substance.'⁵ This Trinity respects plurality in equality. Thus, Augustine nuances, 'the offspring is not less, while the mind knows itself as much as it is; nor is the love less, while the mind loves itself as much as it knows and as much as it is.'⁶ The three, mind, its knowledge and reflexive love, are different, yet intimately equal and united. This passage reveals an important transition. The newly integrated triadic structure of the divine vestiges of humanity captures not only a likeness of God but also 'a certain' image of the Trinity. In other words, Trinitarian alterity is the structure of God's image. Previously, the dyad of likeness and unlikeness presented difference and sameness as composite and opposing tensions of human existence, thus making it difficult to resemble a self-same model of God. With triadic relation, however, following the model of the Trinity where God is three yet one, the interplay of sameness and difference is no longer antagonistic to the image of God, but the very image of God itself. Thus, humanity too bears God's image, literally the triadic constitution of God. What exactly is triadic about this image in humanity? Augustine presents the triad of mind, knowledge and love. This analogy illustrates three clearly distinct aspects of a single mind, where unity and difference interplay dynamically. The analogy is expedient to capture the productive dimensions of alterity. From the unity of the mind, representing the Father, and its self-knowledge, representing the Son, arises love. There is, therefore, a threefold distinction of mind, knowledge and love, within the single operations of a single mind. This is an analogy, of course. The mind is not a substance, in the strict sense of the term. Furthermore, the mind, its knowledge and love are not distinct persons but simply operations of the same faculty. That all analogies ultimately fail to convey the Trinity of God suggests the vestige of the Trinity in humanity is infinitely unlike God. In spite of this, Augustine pursues further analogies to understand the heart of human likeness unto God, namely the structure of alterity. After all, the ideal alterity of the Trinity may be, in some form, present in its vestige on humanity.

The triadic model of the Trinity allows Augustine to reconsider the triadic constitution of humanity's truth in God's image. Truth is no longer self-same unity, as was the case in the dyadic model following the One. In reconsidering the image of God as a triadic vestige of God, Augustine effectively transfers the dyadic framework of falsehood, and therefore the truth of humanity, into a triadic structure after the Trinity. What does this imply? As Augustine continues to wander through the chambers of his memory in search of a perfect vestige of the Trinity, he recognizes the image of God. Closely echoing a passage of *On the Trinity*,[7] Augustine draws an explicit parallel between alterity and the truth of belonging as both being triadic divine images in *City of God*. He writes,

> We indeed recognize in ourselves an image of God, that is, of the supreme Trinity. This image is not equal to God. [The Trinity is that] we exist, and we know that we exist, and we take delight in our existence and our knowledge of it. Moreover, in respect of these three things of which I speak, no falsehood which only resembles the truth troubles us.[8]

This passage offers Augustine's insight into a revised understanding of falsehood and its relation to human identity. Previously, Augustine defined falsehood in *Soliloquy* as 'that which tends to be, but is not'.[9] This formulation of falsehood brilliantly matches Augustine's definition of time in *Confessions*, namely 'the tendency not to be'. On this, Augustine echoes Plato's definition of time in the *Timaeus* as 'a moving image of eternity' (*Timaeus*, 37d). For Augustine, the defining characteristic of time, and of falsehood, is the dynamism towards non-being.[10] By implication, humanity's likeness in the dyadic framework of resemblance implied an inherent passing quality of human life characterized as a falsehood. The falsehood of difference, accordingly, was to be rejected in the quest for the eternal truth of self-same unity. However, in reconsidering the image of God, no longer simply dyadic likeness or difference, in the triadic framework, Augustine writes, 'no falsehood which only resembles the truth troubles us'.[11] Why? With an incorporated structure of alterity, difference is not simply a likeness. Difference is inherent to what it means to be human and, therefore, cannot be discarded. Accordingly, the search for truth is no longer discarding difference but realizing the human constitution in the divine triadic image. In a triadic framework, to find the truth of human identity becomes not a question of mimicry but a question of recognition. The alterity of the divine image is there all along, and the first step towards belonging consists in recognizing this interior structure as God's imprint on humanity. What does it mean to recognize the triadic image of God? It means to recognize the logic of the Trinitarian constitution of human interiority. Augustine articulates recognition of the image of God in *On the Trinity* in terms of two modes of interior reflexivity.[12] The first is reflexive thinking (*se cogitare*), whereby interiority arises as relational difference.[13] The second mode is reflexive knowledge (*se nosse*), where interior presence is unmediated and enduring. Thus, reflexive thinking (*se cogitare*) accounts for difference, and reflexive knowing (*se nosse*) consists of sameness. Accordingly, falsehood is no longer the outcome of difference, as was the case in *Soliloquy*. In *On the Trinity*, the modes of interior alterity reveal existence in the possibility of recognizing difference. The famous Augustinian passage cited earlier, which notably anticipates the Cartesian *cogito ergo sum*, ensues as follows:

For if I am mistaken, I exist. He who does not exist clearly cannot be mistaken; and so, if I am mistaken, then, by the same token, I exist. And since, if I am mistaken, it is certain that I exist, how can I be mistaken supposing that I exist? Since, therefore, I would have to exist even if I were mistaken, it is beyond doubt that I am not mistaken in knowing that I exist.[14]

Whereas Descartes's *cogito* operates as the Archimedean lever for a solipsistic existence, Augustine's *fallor* locates alterity as the foreground of all certainty. Read as a whole, the foundation and truth of human existence in *City of God* lies in recognizing the triadic structure of the divine image by means of constructive fallibility. Hence, truth and falsehood are no longer about difference and sameness, as in the dyadic model. Now truth and falsehood are about presence recognition, according to relational presence. One of these is immediate. The second one is indirect. To the extent that there is direct recognition, there is truth. Conversely, to the extent recognition is mediated, there is falsehood. In either case, the structure of alterity is preserved by the triadic image of God. Furthermore, relation in the triadic structure emerges, fundamentally, not in absolute sameness or difference but in a capacity for God. Augustine therefore defines the image of God as a capability for God (*capax dei*).[15] In reconsidering the structure of belonging according to the Trinity of God, Augustine therefore reshapes alterity into a capacity for divine relation. The image of God as a capacity is the pivot that allows Augustine to focus on relation as the generative force of human belonging. By thinking about human belonging in terms of the Trinity, Augustine discovers the centrality and the implications of relation to preserve difference in identity, just as ontological difference of persons remains distinct within the single substance of a Triune God.

Trinitarian relation

Augustine models the capability for God in terms of relation of alterity in the image of God, according to the relations of Father, Son and Spirit in the Trinity. What is a relation? In answering this question, Augustine turns to Aristotle. This Augustine narrates in the *Confessions*, regretting later that learning was not a pursuit of the truth of God but a mirror of his pride. Augustine recounts, 'when I was about twenty a certain writing of Aristotle had been put into my hands, entitled *The Ten Categories*. What a proud mouthful it was when my rhetoric master at Carthage, and other reputedly learned, rattled off the list of them, though I wonder now what profit that was to me.'[16] At this stage, Augustine was attempting to fit God within the categories of human understanding, and, having easily understood the infamous Aristotelian text, he later regrets his intellectual pride. Augustine continues, 'when I compared notes with other students, who admitted that they had scarcely understood the *Categories* from the most expert masters – masters who not only gave oral instruction but even drew plenty of diagrams in the dust – I found that they were unable to tell me anything I had not already grasped from my private reading.'[17] Years later, Augustine would return in *On the Trinity* to recur to these Aristotelian categories or modes of predication, to make sense of the Trinitarian relations of Father, Son and Spirit. In the *Categories*, Aristotle delineates predicates (τὰ λεγόμενα) or ways of saying or calling things.[18] There are ten categories: (1) substance, (2) quantity, (3) quality, (4) relatives, (5) somewhere, (6) sometime, (7) being in a position, (8) having, (9) acting and (10) being acted upon.[19] Following Aristotle closely, Augustine enumerates the content of the *Categories*. He writes,

> The categories seemed clear enough to me as they spoke of substance (a man, for example) and of accidents inhering in the, such as appearance (what he is like), his stature (how many feet high), his relationship (whose brother), where he is, when he was born, his posture (standing or sitting), whether he is wearing sandals or is armed, whether he is doing anything or whether anything is being done to him; or spoke of any of the innumerable attributes to be found in any of these nine categories, a few of which I have mentioned by way of example, or in the main genus of substance.[20]

Augustine recognizes the centrality of substance and is mostly interested, at this point in his journey, to understand God in terms of them. Eventually, he regrets attempting to use them to grasp God. He writes,

What profit had it been to me? Supposing that these ten predicates covered everything that exists, I mistakenly attempted to understand even you, my God, in terms of them, you who are wonderfully simple and changeless, imagining that you were the subject of your greatness and beauty, and that those attributes inhered in you as in their subject, as they might in a material thing. I did not realize that you are yourself identical with your greatness and beauty, whereas a material thing is not great and beautiful simply because it is that thing, because even if it were smaller or less beautiful it would still be the material thing it is. No, the reading had been no profit to me – a hindrance, rather. My conclusions about you were falsehood, not truth, the figments of my misery, not the firmament of your happiness. As you commanded, so did it befall me: the earth brought forth thorns and thistles for me, and I garnered my bread by much labor.[21]

Initially, Augustine's assessment is that since the properties of God are not different from God, therefore, the categories are not of use to speak about God. The reason for this is, as Augustine notes in the passage, that God is changeless. There are properties, and therefore the categories apply only when there is change. Considered as God, the categories prove of little use. However, this initial attitude towards Aristotle's categories is complicated when thinking about the triad of God, where Father, Son and Spirit are neither properties nor substances. Whereas substance applies to God – and this does not imply God is a substance, but simply that substance can be predicated of God[22] – of the categories, the best denotation of triad is relation. This would prove quite problematic, however, as Augustine continued wrestling with Aristotle. The central categories Augustine borrows from Aristotle to describe the relation of alterity are naturally *ousia* or substance and *ad aliquid* or relation, literally *towards something*. Substance is the divinity of the Trinity, and relation is the difference of persons. For Aristotle, the most basic category is substance. All the other categories are predicates of substance. This means categories (2) to (10) are accidental to substance. Substance is never accidental. Substance is foundational being. In other words, substance can exist without accidents, but accidents only exist in or as predicates or modifiers of a substance. This is what Aristotle suggests. The

Trinitarian debates recognized the divinity of the Trinity as *ousia* or substance. The being of Trinity is one and divine. However, the notion of *persona*, to capture difference, is relation. This poses a problem that reveals the limits of philosophical language. That is, under the Aristotelian scheme, the persons of the Trinity, Father, Son and Spirit, are predicated relations of the divine substance. This has two implications, following Aristotle's principles. First, the relations of alterity are accidents, and therefore not inherent to God. Second, modifications of the divine substance imply consequently divine mutability. However, for Augustine, the three persons of the Trinity are inherent to God, and God is immutable. How, then, does the predication of substance and relation to the Trinity capture triadic alterity while avoiding losing the integrity of difference? Augustine realizes the complexity and importance of this problem in *On the Trinity*. Since human relation as a capability for God (*capax dei*) depends on the status of Trinitarian relation, it was therefore inevitable for Augustine to wrestle with the implications of introducing philosophical language to discourse on Christian revelation.

Aristotle already notes the problematic aspect of relation in the *Categories*. Relation, like all categories, is a predicate. Predication, however, may loosely denote a number of things. In defining the predicates, Aristotle sets the preliminary conditions for satisfying the requirements of relation. He writes,

> we call the following sorts of things toward something [relation]: all those things said to be just what they are *of* or *than* something, or *toward* something in some other way (any other way whatsoever). Thus, what is larger is said to be what it is *than* another (it is said to be larger than something); and a double is said to be just what it is *of* another (it is said to be double of something); similarly with all other such cases (Italics in original).[23]

According to this lose definition, any relation predicates a relative. This raises an important problem for Aristotle because this would imply that at least some relatives are also substances. Yet this would land the contradiction that relatives are always towards something, and absolute or not towards something. To illustrate this issue, Aristotle considers the human body. The head is relative to the arms, yet this does not mean the human being is a relation. Aristotle explains the problem as follows,

> if the [first] definition of things toward something was adequately assigned, then it is exceedingly difficult, or impossible, to reach the conclusion that no substance is toward something. But if, on the other hand, it was not adequately assigned, and things toward something are rather [defined as] *those things for which this is their very being: to be toward another in a certain way*, then perhaps something may be said about the problem [of heads and hands] (Emphasis in the original).[24]

According to this reflection, not all relations imply relatives. In other words, though relation may be loosely predicated of something *towards something else*, this does not always imply there *is* in fact such relation. Aristotle struggled, throughout his corpus, to address this issue. At one point, he revises the definition for this: 'relatives are those things for which being is the same as being somehow relative to something.'[25] Following this adjustment, a relation is nothing other than a relation; it is exactly the relation. Applied to the problem of the body, the hand is not properly a relation because it is not only a hand but also part of a body. This precision helps Aristotle circumvent the possibility of relations that are substances. The unsatisfactory result is an inconclusive set of definitions aiming at avoiding the possibility of having a relation imply a substance. That Aristotle wrestled with this problem indicates a number of important points. First, some relatives may seem like substances. Second, Aristotle is committed to the view that there is no such thing as substantial relatives. Considering the Trinity, where there is unity and triadic difference, Augustine revisits Aristotle's position. That the Trinity implies an immutable substance requires redefining the conditions of predication. Thus in agreement with Aristotle, Augustine accepts that relatives are not substantial but restricts this to the case of mutable substances. Modification, Augustine understood, is an implication of change and time, and therefore in the immutable Trinity it is possible to have a relation that does not modify the substance. By considering the implications of temporality on being, Augustine maintains the Aristotelian definition of relation and preserves the triadic unity of the immutable Trinity. In so doing, he effectively recognizes that mutability is what frustrated Aristotle's predicament. In considering immutable relation, Augustine discovers its generative dimension.

The following passage from *On the Trinity* illustrates that Augustine is conscious of what is at stake in applying Aristotle's categories to a Trinitarian analysis. 'Nothing therefore is said of [God] modification-wise because nothing modifies him, but this does not mean that everything said of him is said substance-wise.'[26] This is, clearly, because God cannot change. Modifications, however, imply change. Augustine continues,

> it is true that with created and changeable things anything that is not said substance-wise can only be said modification-wise. Everything that can be lost or diminished is a modification of such things, such as size and qualities, and whatever is said with reference to something else (*ad aliquid*) like friendship, proximities, subordinations, likenesses, equalities, and anything of that sort; as also positions, possessions, places, times, doings and undoings.[27]

Augustine acknowledges the suitability of predicating substance to speak of God. The reason for this is that substance does not modify God. God is immutable, and therefore, the concept of substance proves appropriate. Augustine is also aware that predicates like relation (*ad aliquid*) are accidents implying modifications of substances. To explain this, Augustine cites mutability. Predicates like relation, when applied to mutable substances, imply modification. In postulating mutability as the determining factor of accidental modification, Augustine departs from Aristotle. In so doing, Augustine opens the possibility to consider the predication of relation as not implying modification when applied to an immutable substance. In other words, the modification of substance is not due to predication so much as to the ontological constitution of the substance of which or, in the case of relation, 'towards which' something is predicated. Augustine effectively revisits the *Categories* of Aristotle, and their Trinitarian applicability emerges in full force in the argument that follows:

> With God, though, nothing is said modification-wise, because there is nothing changeable with him. And yet not everything that is said of him is said substance wise. Some things are said with

reference to something else, like Father with reference to Son and Son with reference to Father; and this is not said modification-wise, because the one is always Father and the other always Son. [. . .] Therefore, although being Father is different from being Son, there is no difference of substance, because they are not called these things substance-wise; and yet this relationship is not a modification, because it is not changeable.[28]

The basic characteristic of God is prior to any predication and is best thought of in negative terms – that is, in terms of immutability. From there, Augustine notes modification implies mutation, and therefore all positive divine predication must preserve immutability. This is the case, naturally, for the predicate substance, following Aristotle. However, Augustine revises the Aristotelian predication of relation when he states that relation is not accidental and, therefore, does not imply modification of God's immutable substance. Augustine avoids transferring the immutability of human relation in applying the category to the Trinity. In the Trinity, the defining aspect of relation is not modification. In human affairs, alterity construed as relation not only modifies but also indeed defines life. What then is such divine immutable relation that defines without modifying triadic divine alterity? Furthermore, what does this imply for the inevitably immutable human capacity for God? Since mutability is the point of departure to understand divine relation, inevitably (eternal) generation is the best way to conceptualize the alterity of divine relation. Relation or the movement towards constitutes an immutable and eternal Trinitarian generation. The best name for this is love since 'God is love',[29] and its paradigmatic expression for Augustine is the incarnate Christ as the Word made flesh. The focus of the incarnation is the becoming of the logos in the flesh. This becoming is the model of a relation that subsists in eternal unity of alterity and grounds the restless movement of human instability. The incarnation provides a relational model for human beings. Christ

> provides a model for us without having a model itself. For it does not imitate another going before to the Father, since it is never by the least hair's breadth separated from him, since it is the same thing as he is from whom it gets its being. But we by pressing on imitate him who abides motionless; we follow him who stands

still, and by walking in him we move towards him, because for us he became a road or way in time by his humility, while being for us an eternal abode by his divinity.[30]

In this passage, the becoming of the incarnation grounds mutable human relations in the abiding eternity of Christ's divinity. Thus, becoming and the temporal illusion previously defined as 'the tendency to not be',[31] in the incarnation, is transformed into a possibility to be transformed by divine relation. The mutability of humanity is the conduit to rest its restlessness in God's eternity revealed as immutable relation in Christ. The incarnation is a promise of lasting and unwavering bonds of relation. Furthermore, the generative becoming of the substance of God's immutable relation is manifested in love as love.

> Thus [Christ] could be a model for those who can see him as God above, a model for those who can admire him as man below; a model for the healthy to abide by, a model for the sick to get better by; a model for those who are going to die not to be afraid, a model for the dead to rise again [. . .] let us love him and cling to him with the charity that has been poured into our hearts through the Holy Spirit who has been given to us.[32]

(In)visibility is the paradigm for the manifestation of generative love. Thus the dynamism of relational alterity is neither modification (accident) nor stability (substance), but incarnational becoming in manifestation. Important for now is the name of relation, which Augustine identifies as love. In God, love endures in the eternal constitutive alterity of triadic unity. For humans, that the relation of love is accidental means love is the modifying or transformative force of becoming. This adaptation of the divine relation of alterity has important consequences for modelling human alterity accordingly, albeit within the horizon of mutability. The creative generativity of love modelled after Christ is the manifestation of the capacity for God. From the passage of interior triadic images to an expression of God's manifestation of Christ in love emerge human relations. The constitution of loving relation is the church. Revisiting relation in Trinitarian alterity therefore allows Augustine to express the capacity for God no longer, or at least not only, as an interior vestige of God but also to articulate its authentic manifestation in the love of community. That the vestige of the Trinity is no longer spiritual but also relational in the incarnation allows Augustine to integrate corporeality in alterity.

The body as relation

What about the body? Does the body also somehow reveal the alterity of God's Trinity imprinted in the human capacity for God, or does Augustine retain the dyadic rejection of corporeal existence in order to avoid anthropomorphism and ensure divine immutability? Or rather, is Augustine able to retrieve the body by reconsidering it from the vantage point of generative relation? Moreover, in this, is not the body also an image of God redeemed in the resurrection of Christ? In the speechlessness of infancy, Augustine observes, the body groans to express and ultimately fails to communicate its longing for God.[33] Augustine recounts how as a child he must have tried, as all children do, 'with groans and various noises and gestures to convey the thoughts of my heart, so that my desires would be known'.[34] The body expresses the otherwise inaccessible depths of the human heart. The body, though not always able to express what it intends to communicate, nevertheless functions as a kind of universal language. He writes of groaning, 'that this is what they intended was evident from the movements of their bodies, which are like a natural, universal language: the expression of the face, the movement of the eyes, the gestures of the limbs, and the tone of the voice all expressing the disposition of the mind concerning the things that it seeks, possesses, spurns, or flees.'[35] Eventually, the groaning of the human body finds its perfect expression in the body of Christ, the church, where the fullness of human affection finds a receptacle and conduit of manifestation. Christ groans in the voice of the Psalms on behalf of the church on the cross. There, the body gains an unparalleled centrality in the thought of Augustine. This view was the produce of ardours thinking and emerged only decades later. Under the spell of the Manicheans early on, Augustine hesitated to ascribe an important place to the body, particularly as somehow related to God or as having a divine origin and role in expressing the image of God. Instead, Augustine focuses on defining the image of God in humanity, following Ambrose, according to the spiritual and immaterial soul. However, upon reconsidering

Trinitarian alterity and its consequence on the centrality of the body of Christ in unravelling generational relation, corporeality suddenly arises with unprecedented magnitude. This brings Augustine to identify the church or the body of Christ as the image of God. In other words, only in considering divine alterity was Augustine able to integrate the body in the constitution of human belonging. Early on, in explaining Genesis, Augustine refuses to concede the corporeal constitution of the divine image in humanity. Instead, invisible interiority is the locus of divinity. He writes, 'And so it is quite unnecessary to ask what God made the man's body from – if, that is, it is now just talking about the formation of the body. That, you see, is how I have heard that some of our people understand the text.'[36] Augustine continues,

> They say that the reason it didn't add "to his image and likeness," after saying God fashioned the man from the mud of the earth, is that now it is only talking about the formation of the body, while the moment when the interior man was being referred to was when it said: God made the man to the image and likeness of God. (Gn 1:27)[37]

Following the narrative of Genesis closely, Augustine relies on the metaphor of formation and mud to describe God's act of creation. The formation is an individuating principle for Augustine. This means things become what they are upon receiving a form, and this, too, is the case for human beings. Furthermore, in the explanation that follows, mud is expedient to discern the body from the soul. Augustine argues that the soul, not the body, bears the image of God. Augustine writes, 'so if, as I am saying, we understand that in this place the man was made of body and soul, it was by no means absurd to give that mixture the name of mud.'[38] The image of mud is a metaphor for the mixture of the body and soul, which constitutes human beings. 'Just as water, you see, collects earth and sticks and holds it together when mud is made by mixing it in, so too the soul by animating the material of the body shapes it into a harmonious unity and does not permit it to fall apart into its constituent elements.'[39] Human beings are like a mixture of water and mud, where water represents the soul and mud represents the body. The image illustrates that although it is easy to separate the composition of mud in words, it is not easy to do so in practice, since mud is a mixture of water and earth. Human beings are therefore a harmonious unity. Thus, in a complicated sense, the soul is the image of God and the body too, insofar as the soul enlivens the body and since the two are mixed. Augustine goes further. He ascribes the form of the body, not only its constitution but also a spiritual sense:

> 'Unless perhaps the fact that the human body is constructed to stand erect, for looking up at the sky avails to support the belief that the body itself was also made to the likeness of God, so that just as that likeness is not turned away from the Father, so the human body is not turned away from the sky as are the bodies of other animals, which are laid out prone on their bellies.'[40]

Without saying that the body is like God, the figure of the body in a sense signifies God. In turning towards heaven, the body is a reminder of the divine traces of the human soul. Augustine goes further. 'And this signifies that our spirit also ought to be held upright, turned to the things above it, that is to eternal, spiritual realities. [. . .] the upright posture of the body there to remind us, that it is above all as regards the spirit that man was made to the image and likeness of God.'[41] The mechanism of signification, operative in these lines, indicates decisively that the figure of the body can be a sign of the divine image. According to Augustine, 'a sign is something which, offering itself to the senses, conveys something other to the intellect.'[42] Considered as a sign, the upright figure of the body conveys the divine vestige of humanity. In this, the body gains unprecedented traction in its important role in conveying the relational alterity of God, constitutive of human belonging. This was an inevitable position to reach in light of considering the incarnation as the paradigm of relation. For this reason, Augustine thereafter considers the effects of immortality on the image of God. As Augustine postulated, relation applies differently to immutable things. That the body only signifies but does not comprise the image of God is not because of a denigration of the body. Rather, it is because complete integration of the body within the alterity of human identity is only possible when the body reaches immutability in immortality. This is why Augustin writes, 'According to this image of the Son to which we are conformed through immortality in the body, we likewise do that which the same Apostle says: "As we have borne the image of the earthly, let us bear also the image of him who is from heaven" [cf. 1 Cor. 15.59].'⁴³ Augustine then explains,

> that is to say, let us who were mortal according to Adam hold fast to this with a true faith and with a certain and firm hope that we shall be immortal according to Christ. For in this way, we can now bear the same image, not yet in vision but in faith; not yet in reality but in hope. From the Apostle was speaking of the resurrection of the body when he said these things.⁴⁴

The immortal body of the resurrection, the suggestion is, bears the image of God. This is the complete conformation after death: a conformation where alterity includes the body because relation is possible in the absence of modification while not implying a substance. Naturally, the model for this is Christ. Augustine writes, 'and yet it is also possible to see in these words of John the Apostle a reference to the immortality of the body. For in this, too, we shall be like God, but only the Son, because He alone in the Trinity took a body, in which he died, rose again, and which He brought to higher things.'⁴⁵ The implication of the resurrection is the transformation of the body into a body like unto Christ's body. This body, later, also acquires an ecclesial dimension. The outcome of the resurrection is the integration of communal belonging, even in renewing the body of believers and enjoining it into the body of Christ.

> For this is also called an image of the Son of God, in which He shall have an immortal body, being conformed in this regard to the image, not of the Father, or of the Holy Spirit, but only of the Son, for of Him alone is it read and received by the most sound faith: 'The Word was made flesh' [Jn 1.14]. And, therefore, the Apostle says: 'Those whom he has foreknown he has also predestined to be conformed to the image of his Son, that he should be the firstborn among many brethren' [Rom. 8.29].⁴⁶

However, the conformation of the body need not wait after the resurrection. Because of the incarnation, it is possible to observe the integration of alterity through Christ on earth. The human capacity for relation is not restricted to the interiority or to the divine contemplation by recognizing the interior divine image. The image of God is oriented towards an external manifestation of community, which Augustine calls the church. The church is, on the one hand, the exterior derivation of internal alterity and, conversely, interiority becomes authentic in the framework of church. Thus, the next important moment in unearthing the divine triadic image and the interplay of alterity consists in locating the corresponding external image in the community of the church. The image of God as the image of the Trinity displays a multidimensional structure, which is no longer restricted to sameness and where alterity is indispensable. For Augustine, the image of God is a vestige of the Trinity, which traces humanity back to God, revealing interior alterity as the architecture for the structure of belonging. Augustine extends this insight to the social structure of belonging in a passage from the *Expositions on the Psalms*, where he sees individual alterity as permeating the social imagination as a tripartite structure of divine images. The first part is humanity, made in God's image. The second image is Christ, the visible image of the invisible God. The first two then converge into yet a third divine image, which is the church. Augustine writes,

> Let us recognize ourselves as your image, and hear for ourselves that word in the Song of Songs, Do you not know yourself, most beautiful of women? (Sg 1.7). This question is put to the Church: Do you not know yourself? What does it mean? Do you not know that you have been made in the image of God, O precious soul of the Church redeemed by the blood of the stainless Lamb?[47]

Considered as part of the church, the individual gains an inherent value.

> Consider how valuable you are, reflect on the immense price paid for you. As we say this verse, let us hope as the psalm hopes: may he make his face shine on us, for we carry God's face upon us. Even as the faces of the emperor are said to be present, so it is with us, because the sacred countenance of God is truly present in his image. [. . .] May your countenance shine forth, and if there appears in me some degree of deformity, may what was formed by you be reformed by you. So then, may he make his face shine on us.[48]

In this passage, Augustine finely interweaves a triadic divine image that includes humanity, Christ and the church into the seamless tapestry, which progressively becomes his doctrine of the *totus Christius* or the Whole Christ. The church as the image of God is the paradigmatic framework of belonging par excellence, where alterity is integral to identity, where diversity is harmonized in the orchestration of unity in the body of Christ, everywhere, and in all times, past, present and future. Speaking of Christ, the image of God, Augustine writes, 'Now, if he is the head, obviously he must have a body. His body is holy church, and she, to whom the apostle says, "You are Christ's body, and his members" (1 Cor 12:27), is also his bride. The whole Christ, head and body together, constitute a perfect man.'[49] The body preserves, and indeed perfects, alterity through unity. In this sense, the church perfects what it means to be human. The church as the Whole Christ unites all difference, but without destroying alterity. The image of God thus functions as the interior and exterior structure of belonging, whereby Augustine harmonizes difference and identity into a comprehensive corporeal whole. The body of the church is the glue that holds aright the triadic structure of the divine image, thus externally mirroring the interior form of the divine Trinity. Accordingly, body is generative relation, for Augustine. This is not the body considered as an individual complex, but the mystical body that is the body of Christ, the church. This ecclesial body has more continuity to the corporeal flesh of Christ than to a simple metaphorical or analogical retrieval thereof. The structure of belonging unfolds in the making of belonging as relation in the body of Christ.

Conclusion

What, then, is the structure of belonging, and is belonging from a distance possible accordingly? The structure of belonging is triadic, modelled after the reconsideration of God as a Triune unity. Specifically, God as Triune implied three important points for Augustine. First, human beings bear a divine vestige of alterity. Second, this vestige is the dynamism of relation. Third, such relational vestige constitutes human alterity. Void of an external point of reference, the dynamism of relation remains trapped within the confines of interior illusion. For this reason, the incarnation of

Christ reveals the paradigm of relation in the church. The church, considered as the body of Christ or the *Whole Christ*, is Augustine's astute approach to charting belonging from a distance. Augustine thus challenges the common belief that church is a result of gatherings. Conversely, belonging from a distance is not a given but only a possibility engrained in the human relational constitution after God's image. Therefore, according to the church as the paradigm of relation, belonging consists in the active manifestation of relation irrespective of presence and absence. By means of integrative relation or incorporation, it is possible to belong from a distance by engaging in the labour of making church. Belonging is about actively manifesting relation as the fundamental mode of human existence and, in so doing, to perform church. This leads to the question, how does Augustine construe the making of belonging and what is the mode of relational performativity from a distance?

3

The making of belonging*

Belonging is possible irrespective of distance because the interplay of the triadic divine alterity is inherent to what it means to be human. In other words, distance, considered as difference, is part of belonging, whether by presence or in absence. The question of what it means to belong from a distance, therefore, is about the making of belonging. What, in other words, occasions belonging in the midst of absence? The previous chapter argued that the church is the paradigm of belonging. Accordingly, the making of belonging consists in incorporation to the church by manifesting relation. Augustine's view of incorporation in the church from a distance is evidenced in a threefold progression. First, in the voice of the Psalms, Augustine recognizes the power of words to capture an otherwise inaccessible depth of affection. Second, the suffering Christ on the cross gives a single voice and accordingly unites the dispersed groaning of all humanity. In the voice of Christ, the body of Christ or the church speaks. Thus, to the extent that human beings voice their suffering through the voice of Christ, the Head of the *Whole Christ*, human beings manifest the church. This results in a model where belonging is becoming. Therefore, the practice of belonging consists in performing church through empathic suffering with others through the single voice of Christ. Belonging at a distance is possible by understanding the suffering of the cross as a redemptive force.

---

* This chapter draws from Pablo Irizar, 'Sensing Dislocated Belonging: Augustine on Becoming Members of the Church as Images of God in the Expositions on the Psalms,' Studies in Spirituality 31 (2021), in press.

The truth of sorrow

Making truth is about making belonging. Belonging is a performative exercise. Following the model of the Trinity, relation is generation, for Augustine. Furthermore, the capacity for God as relation, manifested as church according to the paradigm of the incarnation, makes belonging. Relation manifests the church wherever the church may be, irrespective of distance. To express relation therefore constitutes the making of belonging. How, exactly, does relation make belonging? A point of departure is found in a passage of *Confessions*, where Augustine addresses God: 'For behold, you have loved the truth, because the one who [makes] the truth comes to the light. I am resolved to do the truth in my heart before you in my confession, and to do the truth in my writing before many witnesses.'[1] The enigmatic formulation states that it is possible to make truth. This does not mean that Augustine believes truth is relative, or that truth is without points of reference or conditioned by contingent factors. On the contrary, Augustine clearly believes God is truth, the Truth. The gist of the passage is more subtle. The making of truth occurs in confession and, more specifically, in a confession before witnesses. The gaze of the community makes something of Augustine and, eventually, the gaze of God makes everything out of a dissipated life. The purpose of confession, in other words, is to gather through a unifying story the pieces of the squandering of life and to weave it anew into a coherent tapestry before God and within a single tapestry with others. With the indispensable role of witnesses in the making of the truth of belonging, Augustine's early philosophical hope to know 'God and self, nothing more'[2] suddenly banishes. Without God, and others, life is an incoherent dissipation of failed concupiscence. Therefore, Augustine prefaces the line about making truth by the supplication: 'O you who know me: let me know you; let me know even as I am known.'[3] Making truth is nothing other than making church; manifestation actualizes the most authentic expression of the human capability for God in belonging as church. Church alone fulfils the full potential of what it means to be human. A plethora of affects and human passions, what is most human about being human, when enjoined in consonance and expressed in the one voice of Christ, make belonging. In other words, belonging is performative. Belonging does not simply describe a state of affairs but is the very labour of becoming. This labour passes through the experience of affects and passions, as Augustine recounts from early on in the *Confessions*.

Augustine was a man of passion. Early on in his life, in Carthage, he was fascinated by the plethora of emotions, which spectacles would elicit in him as a young man, and what these sorrows make of the listeners. These spectacles were exterior images of his interior experiences. He writes, 'I was entranced by spectacles in the theaters that were full of images of my own miseries and kindled the fire within me.'[4] The spectacles entranced Augustine. In them, he saw the depth of his own miseries, that is, the desire to indulge in the lamentation of other's sorrow, which Augustine would otherwise not suffer himself. He thus puzzles, why is this? 'Why is it that in the theater someone wants to feel sorrow when he sees lamentable and tragic events that he would by no means want to suffer himself?'[5] There is something enticing about willing to be sorrowful in the suffering of others. Yet, there is something repulsive about lacking the courage to embrace the sorrow and indulge in its pleasure only. The spectators find pleasure in sorrow, yet they would not find pleasure in real sorrow. Augustine calls this madness. He notes, 'Yet the spectators do want to suffer sorrow from these things, and their sorrow is their pleasure. What is this but an astonishing madness? For the more someone is afflicted by such feelings in his real life, the more he is moved by them when he sees them on stage.'[6] The issue with such madness, as Augustine calls it, is that it confuses misery and mercy, thereby insisting, and even applauding, the grief of those who enact them on stage.

> We ordinarily call it misery when someone suffers himself and mercy when he suffers out of compassion with others: and yet what sort of mercy is there in the make-believe of the stage? The audience is not instigated to provide help, but simply enticed to feel sorrow; the greater their sorrow, the greater their applause for the actor who portrays these images. And if those human tragedies, whether historical or fictional, are so portrayed that the audience feels no sorrow, they leave the theater complaining and finding fault; whereas if they do feel sorrow, they remain, rapt in attention and enjoying their tears.[7]

The sorrow of the spectacles is sterile, for it remains inconsequential. Compassion requires suffering with others, but also providing a relief to their misery. This fascination with attitudes towards spectacles reveals Augustine's consideration of the importance of sorrow, which becomes progressively more important.

> So then even sorrows are loved. Surely all human beings want to be joyful. Yet although no one wants to be miserable, still, there is something gratifying about being merciful, and there can be no mercy apart from sorrow. Is it for this reason, this reason alone, that sorrows are loved? And this too flows from the stream of friendship. But where does this go? To where is it flowing? To what end does it run into a bubbling whirlpool of pitch, a monstrous cauldron of foul lusts, its course changed and its path diverted, twisted and cast down from heavenly serenity by its own impetus?[8]

Augustine struggles with finding how sorrows, and pleasure, can maintain a divine orientation. Eventually, Augustin's life in the *Confessions* becomes the stage of the spectacle that calls upon the reader's compassion. The act of confession is the exercise of 'making truth' before God and many witnesses. Thus, the spectacle of grief and mercy arises as the deepest truth of belonging. For this reason, Augustine is the son of Monica's sorrow. Monica, a devout Catholic, appeals to Ambrose, bishop of Milan, to engage with Augustine. Monica would plead incessantly to Ambrose for this,

> she insisted all the more, imploring him with copious tears to see me and engage me in discussion. By now he was a bit angry and fed up. 'Leave me,' he said. 'As sure as you live, it cannot be that the son of tears like these will perish.' And she took this answer, as she often recalled to me in our conversations, as though it had been a voice from heaven.[9]

Somewhat paradoxically, Augustine was ambivalent towards expressing his feelings, especially after his conversion. For example, he was suspicious of music's power to stir affections. On the one hand, music stirs the affections towards God.[10] This Augustine captures in recounting the spiritual and even therapeutic effect of music in his conversion:

> And we were baptized, and all anxiety over our past life vanished. In those days I could not have enough of the

wonderful sweetness of meditating on the depth of your plan for the salvation of the human race. How I wept as your hymns and songs were sung, cut to the quick by the voices of your Church lifted up in sweet music! Those voices flooded my ears, and your truth poured forth as a clear stream into my heart, welling up into passionate devotion; the tears flowed, and it was good for me that they did.[11]

On the other hand, the sensuality of music risks entangling concupiscence in the viciousness of selfish delight for its own sake.[12] Especially after his conversion, Augustine was weary of falling yet again into the frying pan of a cauldron of unholy loves.

The pleasures of the ears had entangled me and enslaved me with great ferocity, but you loosed me and set me free. Now, I admit, I do take some pleasure in the sounds to which your words give life, when they are sung with a sweet and well-trained voice – but not so much pleasure that I am strongly attached to them; no, I can arise and depart when I wish. Nevertheless, these sounds claim a place of some dignity in my heart alongside the meanings they convey, by which they are alive and gain admittance into me, and I scarcely know what sort of place is fitting for them. Sometimes I think I honor them more than is right, when I consider that our hearts are enkindled with the flame of piety more devoutly and more intensely by the very same holy words when they are sung than if they were not sung, and that all the affections of our spirit, in all their variety, are aroused – each in its own way – by voice and song, through some hidden kinship that I do not profess to understand. My mind ought not to be given over to the pleasure of the flesh, lest it grow weak; but such pleasure often leads me astray: sense ought to accompany reason patiently, as its follower, for sense deserves admittance only for reason's sake; but instead sense tries to go first and lead the way. Thus I sin in these matters without being aware of it; only later do I realize it.[13]

There is hesitation, for Augustine: 'Thus I waver between the danger of pleasure and the experience of something wholesome.'[14]

With the passing of time, Augustine understood the importance of affects to make truth in Christ in the voice of the Psalms. The problem, for Augustine, especially in his maturing reading of the Psalms, was not about affects as such but about finding a voice that would accurately articulate human suffering and, in so doing, make something new. For this, human effort is insufficient. Rowan Williams writes,

> Augustine famously describes the impact that the Psalms made in the early days after his conversion: more than once, he uses the language of being 'set on fire' by their words, and he describes how they prompted the expression of his 'most intimate sensations' (*de familiari affectu animi mei* (*Conf* 9.4.8)). Perhaps most strikingly, he can compare the recitation of a familiar psalm with the history of human life (*conf* 11.38). The psalm is a meaningful narrative structure, a history of the soul. And souls *only* have a history in conversation with God, Augustine argues. Without the divine interlocutor, the self is broken and scattered. A perfect knowledge of the self would be like the familiar experience of knowing the whole of a psalm as you sing it (*conf.* 11.41) – but, for us, such experience is not in the normal run of things. What we can do, it is implied, is to imagine a wholeness of experienced history in our lives as if life itself were a text, as if the remembered story of our conversation with God represented part of an intelligible narrative or a single song.[15]

Williams situates identity formation within the interplay of a conversation between the self and God, which in turn produces wholeness through the Psalms. Furthermore, the Psalms articulate belonging by unearthing human sensing. Williams continues,

> The psalmist's voice is what releases two fundamentally significant things for the Augustinian believer. It unseals deep places, emotions otherwise buried, and it provides an analogy for the unity or intelligibility of a human life lived in faith. Here is a conversation with God that has a beginning, a middle, and an end. And in the course of that conversation, the human speaker is radically changed and enabled to express what is otherwise hidden from him or her. Augustine speaks of what the psalm he is discussing (Psalm 4, *Cum invocarem*) 'makes of him' (*quid de me fecerit ille psalmus*): the act of recitation becomes an opening to the transforming action of grace (*Conf* 9.4.8).[16]

In the *Expositions of the Psalms*, Augustine writes,

> we must recognize our voices in him, and his accents in ourselves.... We pray to him, through him and in him; we speak with him and he speaks with us. We utter in him, and he utters in us, the plea made in this psalm.... Let no one, then, on hearing these words, maintain 'This is not said by Christ,' or, on the other hand, 'I am not speaking in this text.' Rather let each of us who know ourselves to be within Christ's body acknowledge both truths, that 'Christ speaks here,' and that 'I speak here.' Say nothing apart from him, as he says nothing apart from you.[17]

In this passage, where Augustine identifies the voice of the Psalms with the voice of Christ, making truth consists in enacting identification by mirroring human affections. The human voice is familiar in the voice of Christ and, conversely, the particularities of the voice of Christ resonate with human experience. This identification is possible in the first place because enjoining the voice of Christ in the Psalms is possible because and only when the speaker is already somehow in Christ. In other words, the voice of Christ is able to voice what human beings fail to otherwise convey. For this reason, nothing can be said, Augustine notes, apart from the voice of Christ. Praying the Psalms is therefore not simply about orchestrating voices and progressively achieving unison in the voice of Christ.[18] Praying is about recognizing the insufficiency of the human capacity to articulate the incomprehensible paradoxes of human suffering. Praying is about giving voice to what escapes understanding and the confines of human language. In prayer, we become deeply aware of belonging in the suffering body of Christ as church. Thus, the Psalms give life to the affects. Conversely, praying the Psalms also gives access to the fullness of human experience, the entry port for which is suffering. Maria Boulding eloquently writes,

> The Church became, for Augustine, the only sphere of experience where an understanding of the psalms' words is possible for the individual. No single person is able to enter personally into all the human experience, and the experience of faith, that find poetic expression in the psalms. Only the person of the Whole Christ, who spans all cultures and bestrides the ages, is sufficient for this, and in this poetic, image-laden mode of discourse the mystery of Christ finds incomparable expression.[19]

This stimulating observation echoes what Athanasius believes is a central and often neglected function of the incarnation. He writes in *On the Incarnation of the Word*, 'For the Son of God became man so that we might become God.'[20] In the process of manifesting God to humanity, Christ is also the mirror of humanity. Christ reveals the suffering and vulnerability of the human condition. Making belonging thus requires a recognition of the fragility of life as revealed in Christ. This recognition is intuitive, for it is the experience of suffering. For this reason, Boulding rightly notes that only the body of Christ, diffused throughout the earth and spanning all times and places, alone contains all possibilities of human experience. Within this wholly inhabited field of experience in Christ's eternal incarnation, humanity finds traces and articulates a longing to become human – that is, a longing to make church. Anyone who pries into the incomprehensible depths of suffering can therefore recognize similar echoes in the voice of the groaning Christ of the Psalms. All human voices are church, in a sense, already before coming to this realization. Coming to this realization is the making of belonging.

For Augustine, suffering is the primordial paradigm to understand the church as the distressed body of Christ. In a passage of the *Expositions of the Psalms* Augustine writes,

> The Church is hungry, Christ's body is hungry. This person who is spread worldwide, whose head is on high and whose limbs are here below – this whole person is hungry. We should hear his voice, her voice, in all the psalms, jubilating or groaning, rejoicing in hope or sighing with love in fulfillment; we should hear it as something already well known to us, a voice most familiar because it is our own. There is no need to make heavy weather over indicating to you who the speaker is. Only let each of us be within Christ's body, and we shall be the speaker here.[21]

The voices of the body, which is the church, seamlessly unite in the unifying voice of Christ. If the hunger, joy and love of the body of Christ are not familiar, this is because we fail to recognize it as our own. This means the fantasy of thinking it is not possible to belong at a distance arises from the inability to recognize the suffering of all humanity as our own, precisely because it is our own. After all, believes Augustine, the separation of distance is really but an implication of the body of Christ being severed and of individuals recognizing and voicing its discomfort as its members. To make truth is the condition for suffering and recognizing it thus results in making belonging. The voice of Christ in the Psalms transforms human existence. Augustine writes, 'without any change in himself [Christ] takes upon himself the creatures who needs to be changed, making of us one single man with himself, head and body.'[22] The transformative force of the voice of Christ on the cross makes belonging, of all people in sorrow, in the church. It suffices to recognize human suffering in the distressed Christ on the cross, and to speak with Christ, who has already spoken before all ages, in the words of the Psalms.

Suffering belonging

Suffering performs belonging. Making truth in suffering, therefore, is about becoming one with Christ in the Psalms. Suffering, then, makes belonging. Four gravitational texts of the New Testament chart how Christ joins the church in suffering through the prayer of the Psalms. These passages undergird identification of the suffering faithful with Christ in the *Expositions of the Psalms*.[23] Indeed, an embedded scriptural orchestration underlies the Whole Christ doctrine.

First, sensing suffering is collective. Augustine grounds this in Col. 1.24, where there is a transfer of suffering and the accomplishment of Christ's suffering in the sufferings of the faithful. Paul writes, 'I am suffering for you, and I fill up in my flesh what is still lacking in regard to Christ's afflictions, for the sake of his body, which is the Church.' In commenting on the Psalms, Augustine writes,

> for he has gone before us as our head, but he follows himself in his body. Look at what the apostle says about Christ suffering in him: That I may fill up what is lacking to the sufferings of Christ in my own flesh. What is he going to fill up? That which is lacking. Lacking to what? To the sufferings of Christ. And where are they deficient? In my own flesh. Could any kind of pain be lacking in that man himself, the man that the Word of God became, the man who was born of the virgin Mary? He suffered whatever it was appointed to him to suffer, and he did

so of his own volition, not under any necessity flowing from sin. It seems that he endured everything possible because when, hanging on the cross, he accepted the final sip of vinegar and said, 'It is accomplished'; and bowing his head he breathed forth his spirit (Jn 19.30). What does that mean – 'It is accomplished'? 'Nothing is missing now from the measure of suffering allotted to me; all that was prophesied of me has been fulfilled.'[24]

Suffering is, first, a reminder that as church, we are not alone. In the pain of suffering lies a promise of belonging.

Second, suffering is transitive. The basis for this is Acts 9.4, which concerns ongoing persecution of the church and Christ's question to the fallen Saul, 'why are you persecuting *me*?' (Acts 9.4). Augustine weaves this into the Psalms as well:

> There still remained sufferings for Christ to undergo in his body. You are Christ's body, Christ's members. Because the apostle was among his members, he said, That I may fill up what is lacking to the sufferings of Christ in my own flesh. We are traveling to the place whither Christ has gone before, but it is equally true to say that Christ is making his way to the place where he has already gone in advance, for though Christ has gone before us as head, he follows in his body. And Christ still labors here, and Christ was suffering here from Saul, when Saul heard the words, Saul, Saul, why are you persecuting me? (Acts 9:4)[25]

This insight is not surprising, and the phenomenon of transitive suffering can be called compassion or the ability to suffer with others. Augustine means, furthermore, that in a sense, suffering is part of a larger salvific mission of Christ in which the church partakes till the end of times. Suffering is therefore inescapable, and, in its redemptive transitiveness, it acquires a meaningful character.

Third, transitivity leads to identity because the suffering of the church is the suffering of Christ, as indicated by Matt. 25.40, where Christ claims, 'whatsoever you did to the least of my brethren you did it to me'. Augustine writes,

> It is the same when your tongue instinctively protests, 'You are treading on me', when it is your foot that has been trodden on.

No one has touched your tongue; it cries out in sympathy, not because it has itself been crushed. Even so Christ is in want here, Christ is a stranger here, Christ is ill here, Christ is confined to prison here. We would be insulting him by saying so, had he not said himself, was hungry, and you fed me; I was thirsty, and you gave me a drink; I was a stranger, and you made me welcome; I was naked and you clothed me, sick, and you visited me. And the just will reply, 'When did we see you suffering all this, and minister to you?' He will say, 'When you did that for even the least of those who are mine, you did it for me.' (Matt. 25.35-37.40)[26]

Augustine suggests that suffering allows for human experience to access the passion of Christ, and therefore, the manifestation of God on the cross. The experience of human vulnerability is nothing short of an encounter with Christ on the way to Calvary.

Finally, Christ promises to be present in the midst of suffering. The permanence of suffering in an imperfect, temporal church assures the presence of Christ therein, based on a promise in Matt. 28.20, 'even to the end of the world'. Augustine writes, 'It is necessary for his body, the Church, to endure temptations in this world, but its consoler is never absent. He has promised, Lo, I am with you throughout all days, even to the end of the ages (Mt 28:20).'[27] Identification is not just descriptive, figurative or analogical. There is also a performative dimension to the act of sensing which effects belonging. Indeed, the prayer of the Psalms incorporates the faithful into the sense of the church. After all, only those who are already in the church can fully pray the Psalms with Christ. Yet, paradoxically, by praying the Psalms, the faithful identifies with the sensing of Christ. In other words, the prayer of the Psalms describes how the faithful belongs in the church. However, if belonging is truly delocalized in the *Expositions of the Psalms*, then the prayer of the Psalms not only describes but also most importantly produces identification with Christ. In delocalized identity, belonging is prior to boundaries so that belonging is becoming. In the same way, the universality of *sensing* is prior to unity: by *sensing* with Christ, *all* become *one* in Christ. Thus, the prayer of the Psalms as a universal expression of *sensing* actively produces belonging in the church. In the *Expositions of the Psalms*, belonging is delocalized becoming and *sensing* is the privileged vehicle of incorporation. Therefore, although sensing captures incorporation, the paradox of belonging as becoming remains. On the one hand, all who suffer, by praying the Psalms, may enter the church. Yet, there is no authentic suffering outside of the church. What model of church membership and belonging captures this paradox?

The imitation of Christ in agony

Suffering is redemptive. By suffering belonging and recognizing ourselves as the body of Christ, the church, the body of Christ, inevitably becomes another Christ. This is the most fundamental identity of belonging in the church and the deepest insight about discovering what it means to be human. On this point, the voice of Christ in the midst of his passion at Calvary echoes the experience of suffering and makes belonging in the church. What does the passion of Christ reveal about what in our suffering throughout the world we make of belonging as church? The answer to this question is in 'the seven words of Jesus on the Cross'. These seven words inspire forgiveness (Lk. 23.34), a promise (Lk. 23.43), revelation (Jn 19.26), desolation (Matt. 27.46/Mk 15.34), discomfort (Jn 19.28), fulfilment (Jn 19.30) and embracing divine providence (Lk. 23.46). These words are the pillars that sustain and define a church in suffering because the suffering body of Christ is Christ in Calvary, suffering on the cross today. By following the words of Christ as accomplished promises in the midst of suffering, the suffering body enacts belonging in the imitation of Christ. The imitation of Christ unto death demands overcoming the speechlessness or infancy of human desolation. Only when we truly become what the words of Christ make of us is belonging truly achieved. From this vantage point, making truth emerges as the revelation of authentic interiority in the church. The truth of belonging consists of enjoining the wounded Christ on the cross. To do this, it is important to recognize, as Augustine writes in the *Expositions of the Psalms*, the voice of Christ as our own. Only on the cross does this voice finally gain complete articulation of suffering in the Word manifested. What do these words say?

The first saying of Christ on the cross reveals the humble truth of human vulnerability. On the cross, Christ prays for the forgiveness of his persecutors: 'Father, forgive them, for they know not what they do.'[28] In commenting on these words, forgiveness is extended to the repentant humble and withheld from the proud. Thus, humility is the condition to become reconciled with others. More importantly, reconciliation by means of humility constitutes belonging. Augustine writes, referring to the persecutors of Christ, 'these people, who had looked upon his mortal body and hounded him, were now joined to his body, the Church.'[29] Augustine continues, 'These penitents were excluded from the number of the proud; and for them the Lord's prayer, offered on the cross, had its full effect.'[30] Humility alone attains the full force of reconciliation with the church. Augustine notes, 'There was but one mind and one heart among them, among these very people who had crucified the Lord.'[31] What is humility? Truth. The truth of humility is, Augustine believes, what caused the persecution of Christ. He writes, '[Christ] dealt confidently, and they could not endure his truthfulness. He had come in humility, he had clothed himself in mortal flesh and had come to die; he had come not to do what sinners do but to suffer what sinners suffer.'[32] The humility of Christ, in taking up the suffering of humanity, thus emerges as the transformed truth of the human condition. By becoming human, Christ is able to enjoin the suffering members of the *Whole Christ* into the church. However, in the midst of suffering, the reality of human life is difficult to accept. Thus, rebellion against the truth of human insufficiency becomes the symbolic killing of human life on the cross. Christ utters the fragility of the human condition, which, in the midst of suffering, humans experienced as an unjust condemnation of forces beyond our control. Hence, writes Augustine, 'they could not endure the truthful condemnations he had uttered, what did they do? They seized him, scourged him, mocked him, punched him, spat at him, crowned him with thorns, hoisted him onto a cross, and finally killed him.'[33] Having rebelled against human nature, forgiveness acknowledges the fragility of human life and thus accomplishes enjoining, yet again, the body of Christ as church.

The second saying of Christ on the cross constitutes a recognition and a promise. On the cross, Christ says to one of the repentant thieves, 'verily, I say unto you today, thou shalt be with me in paradise.'[34] Acknowledging the fragility of his humanity, the 'good thief' secured the promise of a paradise. This promise arises only because of repentance and, therefore, only because of becoming church. Making belonging holds the key to a brighter future. What is this promise and can a promise, in the midst of suffering, provide consolation and even healing? To answer this question, Augustine turns to the figure of the thief crucified next to Christ. The thief was able to recognize Christ. This recognition was a confession of the heart through the lips. When the frail body fails, Augustine goes on to illustrate, only the utterances of the heart succeed in penetrating the truth of reality. While many failed to recognize the promise of Christ, even after witnessing his miracles, the 'good thief' saw the truth of Christ's humility on the cross. Augustine writes, 'the thief was nailed securely in all his limbs: his hands were immobilized by nails, his feet transfixed, and his whole body fastened to the wood. That body had no use of its other members, but his heart had the use of his tongue.'[35] The thief represents all of humanity, echoing Adam who in the Garden of Eden stole the forbidden fruit and thus brought condemnation upon humanity. Furthermore, the thief represents the body of Christ, the church. In the midst of distress and suffering, the church is immobile, appended to the wood of its misery and pain. Only one attitude is possible then: the attitude of confession. Augustine continues, writing of the thief, 'with his heart he believed, and with his lips he made confession.'[36] The confession of the thief, representing the voice of the church, is not one of creed, of praise or of repentance. In this confession Christ speaks on behalf of the church thereby giving a voice to the incomprehensible depths of human affliction. This confession constitutes the 'making of truth'. When the body is paralysed, the voice of Christ gives flesh to the human spirit, nailed to the fragility of its humanity. What follows, from this acknowledgement is a promise. Confession therefore leads to hope. Augustine writes, 'He hoped for salvation as a distant prospect, and would have been content to receive it after a long delay; his hope stretched towards a far-off future, but the day was not delayed.'[37] Hope, as a central mode of belonging, is a recognition of a present struggle resulting in reaching out to a better future. The notion of 'stretching towards' is not simply about projection but about realization. Hope is therefore the effectuation of a promise. Augustine concludes, 'In paradise grow trees of happiness. Today you are with me on a tree of the cross, and today you will be with me on the tree of salvation.'[38] The redemptive value of suffering is accomplished in the promise it holds. The hope in Christ redeems the church today, in the midst of suffering.

The third saying on the cross is this, 'Woman, behold thy son. (Says to disciple) Behold thy mother.'[39] On the cross, Christ entrusts his mother to John's care. This comes just as the soldiers have divided the garments of Jesus by casting lots. The imagery of the wholesome tunic of Christ is an image for the integrity of the church. Even in the midst of suffering, the church remains seamlessly whole. The attitude towards his mother, Mary, is indicative of the accomplishment of the promise of salvation. Earlier, in Canna, notes Augustine, Christ repulses his mother. He writes, 'At that time, then, as he was to perform divine works, he repulsed the mother not of his divinity but of his [human] frailty as though she were unknown to him.'[40] This promise, in the time of divine performance, is contrasted to the frailty of human life. Interestingly, in the midst of suffering, Christ recognizes the affection of Mary. 'But now, already suffering in human ways, he who had become man from her commended her with human affection. For he who had created Mary was becoming known at that time for his power, but now what Mary had borne was hanging on the cross.'[41] The body of Christ on the cross here replaces the image of the tunic. The body of Christ is the church crucified on the cross. The invitation to behold is therefore an invitation to understand that in human frailty, Christ reveals the unity of the church. The fullness of time is revealed in the suffering humanity of Christ. For this reason, beholding Christ on the cross is beholding all of the church, at all times, being redeemed. The identification with the body of Christ on the cross is so strong that Augustine then goes on to describe it as a single flesh in the utterance that follows.

The fourth saying of Christ on the cross reveals the unity of the church throughout the world. On the cross, Christ exclaims, 'my God, my God, why have you forsaken me?'[42] This is the despair of the body of Christ voiced by Christ. The doctrine of the *Whole Christ* arises in this favourite passage of Augustine's. In the passion of Christ, Augustine asks, 'Who is speaking here?'[43] How, Augustine continues, can the vulnerability of human life find a voice in Christ who is God manifest?

> The need to make sense of this forces us to recognize that "Christ" here is the full Christ, the whole Christ; that is, Christ, Head and body. When Christ speaks, he sometimes does so in the person of the Head alone, the Savior who was born of the virgin

Mary; but at other times he speaks in the person of his body, holy Church diffused throughout the world.[44]

Augustine makes a distinction between Christ only as 'Head' and Christ comprising both the 'Head' and the 'body'. The 'body' represents the church. As its Head, Christ without suffering the sin of humanity nevertheless gives voice to his aching body, which is the church. In addition to identifying the body of Christ with the church, a central aspect of the church is diffusion throughout the earth. Distance is not a hindrance to belonging. On the contrary, that the church suffers in unison, wherever the body of Christ is dispersed throughout the world, is evidence of the inherent distance of belonging and of recognizing that when we suffer; we are not alone. Indeed, we suffer only within the church. Thus, suffering is a reminder of belonging. Augustine continues, 'We are within his body, provided that we have sincere faith in him, and unshakable hope, and burning charity. We are within his body, we are members of it, and we find ourselves speaking those words.'[45] Faith, hope and charity ensure experiencing suffering, from a distance, within the body of Christ. Later, Augustine identifies these virtues as denoted by the mysterious dimensions of the cross. Faith, hope and charity reveal, in expectation, endurance and reward, the redemption of suffering. Thus, insofar as we recognize ourselves suffering, we are in the body of Christ, for Christ speaks in us. Yet, as far as we observe faith, hope and charity in the midst of trials, we remain united to the Whole Christ, the church. Augustine powerfully conveys the union of Christ and his suffering church when he challenges, 'is there anything strange in affirming that the one same flesh, the one same tongue, the same words, belong to the one flesh of Head and body?'[46] The answer, of course, is no, just as Augustine states in concluding, 'Whenever you hear the voice of the body, do not separate it from the voice of the Head; and whenever you hear the voice of the Head, do not separate him from the body; for they are two no longer, but one flesh.'[47] Christ suffers so intimately with his body that often, the body as church fails to recognize it and therefore seeks to address its questions by overlooking its answers. The church suffers as one even at a distance, and seeking to gap the distance for its own sake constitutes a failure to recognize that the flesh of Christ in us is suffering in the first place. It is also a failure to recognize that the cry of humanity has been for all ages redeemed in the voice of Christ crying to the Father on the cross.

The fifth saying of Christ on the cross is simple and powerful: 'I am thirsty.'[48] Augustine describes this thirst as the fulfilment of prophecies foretold, for instance, in the Psalms: 'And in my thirst they gave me vinegar to drink (Ps 69.21).'[49] This shows, for Augustine, that the voice of the Psalm is the voice of Christ before the incarnation. Furthermore, on the cross Christ as Head speaks for his body, the church. Thus, the church is thirsty. Just as the Word of God speaks from all eternity, so too in the fulfilment of prophecy Christ on the cross continuously labours for the salvation of the church. Augustine writes, '[Christ] worked our salvation on the cross, so that all the predictions of the prophets might be fulfilled in him.'[50] The thirst on the cross thus represents the ongoing fulfilment of the prophetic promise. In its manifestation, the thirst of Christ on the cross as the thirst of the church in agony reveals redemption is unfolded in the midst of agony and has been so from the beginning of time. The world is in a continuous process of creation and salvation. Augustine notes, 'His Word is what *I was*, what *I am*,' and 'my Father did not just work then when he made the world, he is also working now as he governs the world; accordingly, when he made the world, he made it through me; and as he governs it, he does so through me.'[51] In the eternal fulfilment of prophecies foretold, the voice of Christ is a promise of consolation and healing. In a special way, the cross manifests the fulfilment of the promise. For this reason, Augustine insists that Christ chose the hour of fulfilment. This is true for the incarnation and for his death. Comparing the helplessness of the two thieves before their condemnation, Augustine writes, 'The Lord, however, when he so wished, took flesh in the Virgin's womb; when he so wished, came toward humanity; as long as he so wished, lived his life among human beings; when he so wished, took off the flesh; all this was in power, not necessity.'[52] As the church thirsts, Christ's power is manifested. 'So this then was the hour he was waiting for, not the fated hour but the appropriate hour and the one he chose, so that everything might first be fulfilled which had to be fulfilled before his passion.'[53] The challenge, of course, is to recognize that this promise is already being fulfilled in the midst of pain. Hence, Augustine concludes, 'This in effect is what [Jesus] said – but to whom? To the deaf, the blind, the lame, the sick, who would not even acknowledge the doctor, and, being out of their minds in a kind of frenzy, wanted to kill him.'[54] This means the body, the church, did not recognize itself in its wounds and, upon beholding itself, wanted to destroy itself. Being thirsty consists in recognizing the need for redemption and recognizing, in spite of imminent suffering, that even then, suffering is being unfolded in the mystery of it all. Finally, what is the time of Christ's hour, where the glory of God is revealed? Why must it delay? Why must the body of Christ suffer in awaiting the completion of prophecies fulfilled? The answer is simple, 'Because he was teaching patience, he delayed the demonstration of power.'[55] The thirst of Christ reveals the passion was timely and necessary. Augustine concludes, 'So then, if he had not been willing to suffer, he would not have suffered; if he had not suffered, that blood would not have been shed; if that blood had not been shed, the world would not have been redeemed. So let us be grateful both to his divine power and to his compassionate weakens.'[56] In a sense, the prophecy is fulfilled and not. Augustine explains this in the following words of Christ.

The sixth saying of Christ on the cross is a declaration of accomplishment: 'It is finished.'[57] What does it mean? To explain this, Augustine introduces Col. 1.24: 'That I may fill up what is lacking to the sufferings of Christ in my own flesh.'[58] On the one hand, Christ has suffered what Christ had to suffer to fulfil the promise of salvation, and so, for Christ, it is all finished. The power of Christ is manifested in the fullness of time on the cross. Augustine writes, 'He suffered whatever was appointed to him to suffer' and, this time Christ speaking, 'nothing is missing now from the measure of suffering allotted to me; all that was prophesied of me has been fulfilled'.[59] On the other hand, however, the citation from Paul suggests there remains, even after Christ, and unto today, suffering that is lacking and therefore the need to fill it in the flesh of Paul, in our flesh today. To explain this, Augustine returns to the doctrine of the 'Whole Christ'. As the Head, Christ has completed his suffering. In the flesh of his members, the body, which is the church, suffering remains. Suffering therefore happens in the church as the ongoing redemptive plan, unfolding in time, from all eternity. This suffering only truly makes sense, when considered as completing, in the flesh, what Christ has achieved as the Head. All of suffering converges in the redemptive plan of salvation, for Augustine. He concludes, 'We are travelling to the place whither Christ has gone before, but it is equally true to say that Christ is making his way to the place where he has already gone in advance, for though Christ has gone before us as head, he follows in his body. And Christ still labors here.'[60]

In a most mysterious sense, in the midst of suffering lie hidden, Augustine suggests, the redemption of all suffering and the ongoing labour of Christ's passion from all eternity. Furthermore, in this suffering lies the deepest truth of the unity of the body of Christ, and indeed, its purpose: to complete the work already accomplished on the cross. Augustine uses the example of the martyr Stephen, stoned to death, to illustrate this in the death of Christ on the cross. This corresponds to the final words of Christ on the cross.

In the final words of Christ on the cross before death, he says, 'Father, into thy hands I commit my spirit.'[61] Augustine understands this as a concrete and indeed the ultimate way to follow Christ and in so doing to become church. The example for this, following Paul in Acts, consists in giving up one's life in order to fill what is lacking in the sufferings of the body of Christ. Augustine writes, 'Observe the man following in the Lord's footsteps. Christ on the cross: *Father, into your hands I commend my spirit* (Lk 23.46); Stephen under the hail of stones: *Lord Jesus, receive my spirit* (Act 7.59). [. . .] how could this man not be where the one he had followed was, where the one was he had imitated?'[62] The words of Christ on the cross converge in the life of the martyr Stephen who, in imitating Christ, becomes the body of Christ, the church.

The sayings of Christ on the cross offer a tangible reflection of human experience. With his dying breath, Christ reveals the redemptive promise inherent in the expression of the humanity of humanity. Accordingly, even in the agony of the cross, the imitation of Christ is possible because the incarnation is a sacrament not only of God's divinity in Christ but also of humanity's most authentic form of vulnerability: an agony that redeems in the making of church. To be as Christ is to become church, and to become church is to make all things new. Accordingly, manifestation presupposes a passage from invisibility to visibility. For this reason, in a peculiar passage of *On the Trinity*, Augustine calls the incarnation a sacrament:

> to balance this double death of ours the savior paid in his single one, and to achieve each resurrection of ours he pre-enacted and presented his one and only one by way of sacrament and by way of model. For he was not a sinner or godless, and so he had no need to be renewed in the inner man as though he were dead in spirit, or by regaining wisdom to be called back to a life of justice. But being clothed with mortal flesh, in that alone

he died and in that alone he rose again; and so in that alone he harmonized with each part of us by becoming in that flesh the sacrament for the inner man and the model for the outer one.[63]

The incarnation offers a model to ensure the continuity of distance and separation and the unity of the body of Christ. Augustine insists on the twofold function of the incarnation. First, as a hidden sacrament or mystery, the incarnation appeals to the inner suffering of human beings. However, this interiority is not isolated and fragmented. In the body of Christ, the church, the interiority of agony also acquires an exterior model. This is the second function of the incarnation. The sayings of Christ on the cross offer this exterior model. In following Christ on the cross, therefore, the church is able to integrate the interiority and the exteriority irrespective of distance. This is, in fact, what the death and resurrection of Christ achieve, namely, an inseparable unity of distance and belonging. The making of the truth of belonging is therefore a manifesting process that unites the interiority of suffering with the exteriority of the church in the suffering Christ on the cross. The imitation of Christ is about becoming the body of Christ and about manifesting belonging as church, diffused throughout the earth. To imitate Christ is to attain the unity of many as one in spite of distance.

Conclusion

Belonging in the midst of absence, and even in spite of presence, is the result of the ability to voice the otherwise mysterious depths of human passions and affection. This is possible by enjoining our voices to the voice of Christ in the Psalms. The unison of the church's prayer in groaning as suffering body of Christ in the voice of the crucified on the cross effects belonging. Belonging is about performing church in and through suffering. In suffering alone is the mystery of interior alterity revealed as dynamic capacity for relation with others through Christ. In this sense, belonging is the work of compassion – that is, the practice of suffering with others. However, Augustine does not reduce belonging to solidarity, which is what causes many to seek presence as an antidote to the loneliness of distance. On the contrary, for Augustine, belonging is about reconfiguring suffering. Compassion is about making belonging. For this reason, belonging at a distance is possible only by assuming that the suffering of Christ on the cross has a redemptive power that roots and efficaciously transforms reality. Augustine thus avoids, on the one hand, reducing the role of the church to a camp of communal solidarity longing to overcome distance and once again find belonging. On the other hand, for Augustine, making belonging from a distance does not only fulfil a psychological need at best or produce a spiritual psychosis at worst. The possibility of making belonging, therefore, requires an ontology of invisibility, which is the primary mode of suffering from a distance, with others, yet possibly in the absence of others also.

4

The manifestation of belonging

Belonging from a distance is possible only in the suffering that occurs in the incorporation of the body of Christ, diffused throughout the earth. Therefore, in a profound metaphysical sense, distance is a requirement for belonging. Furthermore, in partaking in suffering, as the body of Christ, from a distance, the church completes the redemption already achieved by Christ on the cross. The true difficulty in belonging lies not in distance but in invisibility and in construing a performative paradigm of manifestation. Often confused with distance during the pandemic, invisibility poses a problem, first, in that the presence of others is not necessary for belonging. Because of this, once the manifestation of suffering as church achieves belonging, it is difficult to recognize it. Invisibility also poses a problem of recognizing, in the manifestation of suffering, the accomplishment of an already accomplished redemption. The difficulty with recognizing belonging as belonging within a redemptive framework of suffering often leads to losing faith in the invisible. Yet, in the pandemic, the invisible has become the most powerful driving force of daily life – that is, the invisible reality of a deadly pathogen which brings death without discrimination. For this reason, also, faith in unseen belonging and in unseen redemption also. The primacy of perception and manifestation has been lost. However, Augustine roots belonging in distance – physical distance within the diffused body of Christ, and temporal distance from the redemptive passion of Christ on the cross. Does this therefore imply that the cross is simply a symbolic representation without any real import besides identification? In other words, what exactly is the suffering value of the figure of the cross? What does it do for a suffering world in the midst of a deadly pandemic? Is it simply a sign of comfort? In addition, what comfort is there in a brutal death of God's Son? This question touches on the core of what, if anything, the passion contributes to the pressing crisis of invisibility. Can the cross truly redeem the human capacity to trust what is not visible? Augustine offers a masterful answer to this question by articulating a powerful paradigm of manifestation. He writes, 'from the depth which you cannot see rises everything that you can see.'[1] This is not simply a question of perception. All of reality rises from the invisible. The only sure path to seeing anew, and therefore recovering the essence of belonging as a redeemed church in the midst of suffering, lies in understanding this mechanism of manifestation. By remaining attuned to the reality of distance, the invisibility of a church in absence unfolds as the truest expression of belonging. Augustine comes to articulate the paradigm of manifestation upon first understanding the dialectic of invisibility. He then posits dimensions as signs of manifestation. Finally, Augustine analyses the cross as the performative paradigm of manifestation.

Invisibility and manifestation[2]

The dialectic of invisibility arises, for Augustine, within the problematic relationship between the immaterial soul and the material body, an invisible spirit and a visible flesh. Dimensions are the starting point of visibility. Tertullian conceived the soul as a corporeal reality and therefore had no difficulty explaining how the soul, like the body, though invisible, is contained within space. In other words, for Tertullian the passage of invisibility does not imply a passage of immateriality. The same is not the case, however, for Augustine. Augustine upholds an immaterial account of the soul and therefore is confronted with the problem of having to describe how matter relates to immateriality and, more importantly, in articulating a performative paradigm of manifestation. How, in other words, is the invisibility of belonging manifested at distance? What roots the manifestation of belonging in the absence of presence? What ensures belonging is not reduced to a disincarnate idea at best and to a delusion at worst? Only a performative paradigm of manifestation can overcome this problem. And it is all rooted in Augustine's inheritance of applying dimensions as the locus of visibility, from Tertullian, and having to apply them in a philosophical framework where the soul is spirit, not matter. This came in hand with a larger question, namely, how is an incorporeal God, after whom the soul is spiritual, manifested in a corporeal world. For Augustine, dimensions mark the passage from invisibility to visibility. In this passage, things come to be. In engaging with this question, Augustine finds in the figure of the cross the ultimate paradigm of manifestation where 'from the depth which you cannot see rises everything that you can see'.[3]

Tertullian insists that God creates the soul not from pre-existing matter while affirming, following the Stoics, that even the spiritual soul is corporeal. This is because, as Dunn notes, 'something incorporeal could not give life to the incorporeal body'.[4] In response to Tertullian, Augustine draws from Neoplatonism and pivots to infer, from the presence of dimensions and geometrical shapes, that the soul is incorporeal and therefore eternal. Augustine is concerned with discussing the relationship between quantity or magnitude and eternity, especially as related to the soul. How do the dimensions of the body restrict the soul? The earlier appearance of dimensions in the work of Augustine occurs in the *Soliloquy* where, in conversation with a fictive character called Reason, Augustine concludes the soul is immortal because it contains immortal truth. The argument is based on, and well illustrated by, the question of dimensions of geometrical figures. Whereas Tertullian argues the dimensions of bodies too are the dimensions of the soul, Augustine shows the presence of geometrical dimensions in the soul as a case of truth which is immortal, so too the soul must be immortal. For the truth of geometrical figures not to be in the figure or the figure in the truth, the line would have to be conceived as something other than what it is: a length without width. The untrue imitates what it is not. Yet, Augustine notes, geometrical shapes are self-same and therefore require no other truth. Therefore, geometrical shapes show truth is in the soul. He first notes the presence of truth in the mind: 'R.—There is no need, then, to inquire about dialectic. Whether geometrical figures belong to Truth, or Truth is in them, no one doubts that they are contained in our minds, so that necessarily Truth is in our minds.'[5] From there, Augustine infers the soul too, which is inseparable of the truths it holds, is likewise unquestionably true. He writes, 'But if any scientific discipline is in the mind inseparably, and Truth cannot perish, why, pray, should we doubt concerning the everlasting life of the mind because of our familiarity with death? Has the geometrical line or square or circle anything else to imitate in order that it may be true?'[6] To these rhetorical questions, Reason's interlocutor concedes the truth of geometrical figures is undifferentiated from the figures themselves that the mind considers. Therefore, truth is in the mind, 'unless a line is other than length without breadth, and a circle is other than a line drawn round a centre and always equally distant from the centre'.[7] However, clearly, a line is breath without length, and a circle is a radius equidistant from its centre. The argument for the eternity of the soul is complete. The immortality of truth found in the geometrical figure is also found in the soul where the figure is contained. This proves Augustine's hypothesis that the soul is immortal if it is to contain immortal truth. Hence, on the one hand, the reception of Tertullian's questions in Augustine's early work is quite innovative. Yet, as this passage of *Soliloquies* suggests, Augustine continues to contend with a debate on the constitution of the soul. Like Tertullian, Augustine wrestles with the possibility of existence in relation to corporeality, in both God and the soul. However, whereas Tertullian focuses on explaining the body of God and soul, Augustine focuses on how an incorporeal being relates to corporeality. Tertullian postulates a corporeal soul to explain the genesis of the soul from God, whereas Augustine argues for an incorporeal soul to demonstrate the immortality of the soul. Underlying these competing positions is the argument for the passage from invisibility to manifestation. In other words, how do the dimensions of the body manifest the soul? For Augustine, dimensions, irrespective of bodies, are the locus of truth. This matures in his later appreciation of the dimensions of the cross as the locus of divine manifestation.

A related question arises when considering God. How does God, who is invisible and immaterial, act in the material and visible world? Augustine deals with the question of God's creative act much like Tertullian – that is, in terms of dimensions and corporeality. In *On Music*, Augustine notes that the elements that produce everything cannot come from nothing, some argue. Augustine questions that something as low as the earth can be the source of everything that exists harmoniously. The process of this passage from nothingness into existence rejoins the figure of the cross in the passage from invisibility to visibility. It is difficult to consider God's creative act from nothing, and therefore, the analogy of the passage from indivisibility to visibility offers the best conceptual analysis. As before, Augustine refers to the unmistakable truths of geometrical figures. Augustine is particularly interested in how figures emerge from the analogical nothingness of a point. He writes that in a figure, 'any of its particles, however small, from an indivisible point is extended necessarily into a line, receives thirdly the surface, and fourthly the volume by which a body is complete'.[8] The paradigm of manifestation in this analysis consists of the act of extension. Without extension, a point, representing the nothingness from whence all being emerges into existence, remains invisible. This invisibility is not simply a failure of perception. It represents non-existence. For things to be perceived, in other words, they must exist, and they exist, furthermore, because they are extended into the horizon of visibility. From these observations, Augustine concludes that 'if we remove these dimensions from the earth, it becomes nothing. For this reason, God almighty produced the earth, and the earth was produced from nothing.'[9] There is no existence without dimensions, and, by implication, dimensions are the locus of visibility in God's creative act. Yet, since the act of extending things into existence requires divine agency, Augustine postulates that there must be 'a movement outside of time must precede all order of creation'.[10] This movement outside of time fulfils two important conditions. First, it engenders time. After all, Augustine defines time as an extension. To extend nothingness into being implies the manifestation of time. Second, that all things become visible is possible not by a sequence of divine and temporal acts. This would subject divine agency to the confines of mutability. Rather, the metaphorical movement of time is the acknowledgement that things come into existence, and therefore to the horizon of visibility, in that they are perceived by God. Thus, creation reveals for Augustine that the passage from invisibility to manifestation consists in a movement that is extension and perception. On this salient point, Augustine rejoins Tertullian's concerns over the mode of God's creation and insists on the doctrine of *creatio ex nihilo*.[11] Unlike Tertullian, for Augustine, God must not be corporeal and must be outside of creation to create *ex nihilo* and in so doing to set all the elements into motion. Movement into existence arises progressively with the coming of dimensions. Augustine delineates this progression as he rhetorically asks,

> from whence comes this arithmetic progression form the first to the fourth? And from whom also the equality of the parts,

which are found in the line, surface and volume? And from whence the rational analogy, by which has the relation between the indivisible line, and also the surface to the line, and the volume to surface? From whence if not from the sum eternal principality of the numerical values, of proportion, of equality and of finality?[12]

Thus, dimensions play an ontological role in ensuring the existence of things and their fourfold progression into visibility, from a dot to a line, to a surface, to a volume, which is corporeality. The creative act of God shows, for Augustine, that underlying the paradigm of manifestation in God's creative act is a dynamic ontology of becoming. Augustine does not reduce manifestation to (human) perception. Rather, manifestation follows a complex unfolding of reality which ultimately depends on God's creative perception. Returning to the paradigm of manifestation, creation is the grounds for how, eventually, 'from the depth which you cannot see rises everything that you can see'.[13] All things visible necessarily proceed, in an ontological fashion, from what is invisible.

In maturing reflection, Augustine integrates his views on God's creative act to return to the question of how the soul and body relate. In addition, this, in turn, leads Augustine to articulate God's mode of creation as an eternal act of presence, encompassing the perception of 'all in all'. In response to a number of questions brought to his attention for an answer, Augustine writes, 'because of the four well-known natures from which [the body] is composed – dry, wet, cold and hot – and because the movement from a point to width, from width to breadth, and from breadth to height makes for the sodality of the body.'[14] Augustine insists on the immortal aspect of the body but wrestles more overtly with the question of how the soul relates to the body while extending beyond it. Augustine first makes the uncontentious observation that bodies must have *three* dimensions, namely length, weight and height.[15] He then unprecedentedly identifies height (*altitudo*) as the most essential of the three. The reason for this is based on perception. He writes, 'the dimension which makes it possible for the interior of a body to be an object of thought, or, if the body is transparent as glass, the object of sense perception. In my opinion, at least, if you take this dimension away, bodies can neither be perceived by the senses nor be thought of at all as bodies.'[16] The purpose of this statement is to frame the difficult relation between the soul and body by showing how by means of only height preserved in sense perception the incorporeal soul can perceive corporeal objects. This helps establish the possibility for the existence of immaterial aspects such as justice, and therefore the possibility of an immaterial soul and leads to the question of how the soul and the body relate.[17] Augustine considers this relationship using the metaphor of wind, which may suggest the body is still invisible, but nevertheless a body.[18] While Augustine concedes that the spirit can be contained within the body in a sense like wind in a bottle, unlike wind in the bottle, Augustine contends, the soul extends beyond the body, thereby proving the soul is immaterial.

> A. Is the soul inside the body only, like the contents of a bottle, so to say, or only on the outside, like a covering, or do you think it is both inside and outside? [. . .] E. I think it is both inside and outside. For, unless it were inside, there would be no life inside of us, and unless it were on the outside, it could not feel a slight prick on the skin [. . .] the soul is as large as the spaces of the body allow.[19]

The ability of memory to consider things spatially absent illustrates, according to Augustine, how the soul immaterially extends beyond the body, which contains it. He writes, 'Since your soul is here where your body is, and does not extend beyond the space of the body, as the previous proof made clear, how is it that it sees all these things?'[20] Again, 'How great therefore, the depth, the width, the immensity of the soul that can hold all these things, although our previous proof seems to show that the soul is only as great as the body.'[21] The soul is, therefore, 'a certain kind of substance, sharing in reason, fitted to rule the body'.[22] This is Augustine's early attempt at wrestling with Tertullian's question of how an incorporeal soul relates to a body. At this point, Augustine is quite Plotinian, a position that will change over time. For instance, Augustine returns to the question in *On the Trinity*.

> All these of course conceived it to be mortal, since whether it is body or some arrangement of body, it cannot continue immortally

> [. . .] seeing that it is life that animates and vivifies every living body. These tried, as best as each of them could, to prove that mind is immortal, since life cannot lack life [. . .] something whose part in a localized space is smaller than the whole [. . .] they call every substance, or at least every changeable substance, body, while knowing that not every changeable substance is contained three-dimensionally [*longitudine et latitudine et altitudine*] in localized space [. . .] mind is in nature both substance and not body, that is that it does not occupy a smaller space with its smaller part and a bigger space with its bigger one.[23]

The same problem, initiated by Tertullian, Augustine applied not only to consider how the incorporeal soul relates to the body but also to how God relates to place. Augustine notes, 'God is not in a place, for that which is in a place is a body, but God is not a body. Therefore he is not in a place.'[24] What, then, is the relationship between God and the world? How does the world proceed into the horizon of manifestation by means of God's creative act?

> And yet, since he is and he is not in a place, all things are in him rather than he himself being in some place, although they are not in him as if he himself were a place. For a place is in space because it is defined by the length, breadth and with characteristic of a body. God is not like this. Everything, therefore, is in him, and he is not a place.[25]

The thesis, in the opening lines, is counter to Tertullian. It is possible for Augustine to exist and yet be incorporeal, like God. This raises the difficulty as to how God can be in a place at all, if all place is constrained by corporeal dimensions. How can God, who is incorporeal, be 'all in all'?[26] The solution for Augustine is that God is in no place. Rather, all is in God who is not a place – a similar reasoning applies to his views of time and eternity. Interestingly, the omnipresence of God here denoted is present in gnostic and early Christian interpretations of the figure of the cross at Eph. 3.18 but not in Augustine's own interpretation. In light of this, Eph. 3.18 is about not only predestination and grace but also dimensions and wrestling with the corporeal manifestation of an incorporeal God. For this, Augustine's interpretation of the figure of the cross as a paradigm of manifestation offers a solution:

'from the depth which you cannot see rises everything that you can see.'[27] God's omnipresence is not about containment in a place but about maintaining existence under an eternal creative gaze and, furthermore, about manifesting the invisible accordingly. The tool to do this, of course, is the cross, where Christ, the 'visible image of the invisible God',[28] reveals the inscrutable mystery of God. The invisible, for Augustine, is integrally part of the visible and is the root of all that is visible. Accordingly, the figure of the cross, in its depth and height specifically, constitutes the paradigm of manifestation par excellence, whereby quite fittingly, humanity encounters God in Christ, the visible image of the invisible God. The figure of the cross offers a paradigm of manifestation because, for Augustine, in the manifestation of invisibility, dimensions operate as signs.

Dimensions as signs

John Calvin scornfully calls Augustine's interpretation of the figure of the cross at Eph. 3.18 'sublime'.[29] The locus of divine manifestation is the figure of the cross because, progressively, dimensions of a figure function as signs for Augustine. Thus, the figure of the cross eventually functions not only as a symbol but also mainly as a sign. Hence the possibility of thinking of the cross as the paradigm of manifestation. All depends on the premise that dimensions function as sign. For Augustine, dimensions are rooted in signs such that the body is the locus of signification, which reveals God's *performative* presence, especially by signifying redemption in the church.

First, dimensions reveal signs. Already early on, in *The Magnitude of the Soul*, Augustine relies on dimensions to locate signs at the overlap between the invisible soul and the visible body. Concerned with showing that the soul is without dimensions, and therefore immaterial, Augustine intriguingly postulates that signs are the foundation of dimensions. Signs are visible but without extension, not requiring corporeality, yet accessible to the mind and body. Inceptive within the dynamism of the (in)visible relation of body and soul lies hidden the mechanism of signification. The argumentative thrust for this view ensues as follows. Augustine first makes the uncontentious observation that bodies must have *three* dimensions, namely length, weight and height.[30] He then unprecedentedly identifies height as the most essential of the three: 'the dimension which makes it possible for the interior of a body to be an object of thought, or, if the body is transparent as glass, the object of sense perception. In my opinion, at least, if you take this dimension away, bodies can neither be perceived by the senses nor be thought of at all as bodies.'[31] In rendering the interior of a body visible to the senses and to thought, height operates as a means of signification. Height is the most essential dimension because it visibly signifies (in)visible corporeality. As of yet, whether this signification is expressionist or performative remains uncertain; Augustine is solely interested in stating that dimensions imply extension and corporeality. This raises the question as to whether the soul is a body or whether it can exist without dimensions. To answer, Augustine compares the soul to air and tentatively suggests that the body, like air, is contained in the body and is therefore with dimensions. He notes that although bodies necessarily have dimensions, not all things without dimensions are nothing, such as justice. So too, the soul is something without dimensions. Augustine rhetorically asks, 'If justice, therefore, is not any of these things [neither long, nor wide, nor anything I can think of like that], and yet is not nothing, why do you think that the soul is nothing, if it has no length?'[32] The discussion continues in considering the soul as air because like the soul, air is like a body, but also unlike it. 'If we admit that even the wind is a body, I cannot deny that the soul seems to be a body, for I think it is something like the wind.'[33] Wind is air in motion with great dimensions. It seems like a body, but is it? The soul exists only in the body. 'A. Is the soul inside the body only, like the contents of a bottle, so to say, or only on the outside, like a covering, or do you think it is both inside and outside?'[34] To this, Augustine's fictive interlocutor Evodius responds, 'I think it is both inside and outside. For, unless it were inside, there would be no life inside of us, and unless it were on the outside, it could not feel a slight prick on the skin.'[35] Augustine concludes: the soul is 'as large as the spaces of the body allow'.[36] Comparing the soul to air suggests the soul is where the body is, and that the soul does not extend beyond the body.[37] However, Augustine's consideration of memory shows the soul's ability to extend beyond the body. Accordingly, the soul is also in a fundamental way unlike air. Augustine asks, 'Since your soul is here where your body is, and does not extend beyond the space of the body, as the previous proof made clear, how is it that it sees all these things?'[38] Memory sees, by remembrance or imagination, what is beyond the confines of the body. Thus, the soul remembers by extending beyond the body. Augustine writes, 'How great therefore, the depth, the width, the immensity of the soul that can hold all these things, although our previous proof seems to show that the soul is only as great as the body.'[39] The soul is therefore not a body, nor contained in a body, nor confined to a body; rather, it relates to the body but extends beyond the body, and the analogy with wind fails because wind is always fixed within a space because it has dimensions. The soul is therefore unlike air and does not have dimensions. This does not mean the soul remains unrelated to dimensions, especially when considering that the soul somehow stores images of corporeal objects. This raises the problem, how does a dimensionless and incorporeal soul contain dimensions of corporeal things? The answer Augustine advances is deceptively simple: by means of signs. Augustine's response, fully developed years later, relies in this early dialogue on defining length and its relation to signs. Independent of the other dimensions, without which a body cannot be, length is incorporeal. Length is a line only found in the mind and is therefore an extension without body. By introducing the incorporeality of dimensions, Augustine undergirds the possibility for the extension of the soul beyond materiality, thereby bridging dimensions and the (in)visible, especially where 'a mark without parts' constitutes a sign.

> This, then, which I see you now understand, is the most excellent of all our findings, since it completely excludes division. It is called a point when it occupies the center of a figure. But, if it is the beginning of a line, or even lines or their end, or even when it marks something that must be understood as having no parts without having become the center of a figure, it is called a sign. A mark without parts is a sign; a mark occupying the center of a figure is a point. Thus, every point is also a sign, but not every sign is a point.[40]

Length is incorporeal and, when construed without parts in the mind, that is, as a point, length functions as a sign. The signifying power of the incorporeal length (or point) explains why things stored in the soul's memory may overcome corporeal extension. There is more and better. Augustine then postulates that signs are the basis of dimensions, which proceed from length and from corporeality. He continues,

> The length of a line is the foundational unity of dimensions and sign is prior to it. I see that width needs length; otherwise it could not be understood. I notice further that length does not need width for its existence, but without a sign it could not exist. The sign, however, clearly stands by itself and needs none of these.[41]

Augustine concludes: 'it seems to me to be a certain kind of substance, sharing in reason, fitted to rule the body.'[42] The soul is superior to the body in an ontological sense of precedence in that the dimensionless soul operates as a sign, and the hinge of (in)visibility, visible first through length and extending throughout the manifestation of the body. Furthermore, sign emerges as constitutive of dimensions and manifestation. In other words, sign is inherently operative in the functions of the memory but also, and more importantly, in *all* corporeal manifestation. By now, Augustine begins to subtly hint at the inherent performativity of signification. This much is clear: dimensions are the visible manifestation of invisible realities and the body – union of flesh and spirit, at once visible and invisible – is the locus of signification.

Having established that dimensions operate as signs, Augustine then identifies the body as the locus of signification. Augustine elucidates how signs signify at the juncture of the manifestation of (in)visibility in exploring the embodied relation between the soul (immaterial/visible) and the body (material/visible) in Book X of *On the Trinity*. Accordingly, signification converges in the embodiment of (in)visibility, where flesh and spirit mysteriously unite within the framework of dimensions. Augustine first rehearses various opinions on the material composition of the soul, 'All these of course conceived it to be mortal, since whether it is body or some arrangement of body, it cannot continue immortally.'[43] He then notes the immaterial interpretations where the soul is life, 'seeing that it is life that animates and vivifies every living body. These tried, as best as each of them could, to prove that mind is immortal, since life cannot lack life.'[44] In the mortal views of the soul, there are four elements, and the immortal ones postulate a fifth, the material of heaven.[45] Augustine thinks the fifth material element is bodily, so the arguments for the soul's immortality, like opinions on the contrary, ultimately fail. Either the body of the soul, considered as a fifth element is 'something whose part in a localized space is smaller than the whole',[46] in which case the soul is reduced to body, merely a part of the whole and not the whole; or else 'they call every substance, or at least every changeable substance, body, while knowing that not every changeable substance is contained three-dimensionally [*longitudine et latitudine et altitudine*] in localized space',[47] in which case the soul may occupy a larger space than the body. For Augustine, 'mind is in nature both substance and not body, that is that it does not occupy a smaller space with its smaller part and a bigger space with its bigger one.'[48] From this, he concludes, the soul is not restricted by dimensions but wholly occupies dimensions, not as confined body, nor merely as extended substance, but as *fully* embodied three-dimensional substance. The three dimensions thus denote embodiment. The sign and signified, the visible and the invisible, converge in the place and space of the body, even if the soul extends beyond its confines. The body is accordingly the locus of active signification. By its very constitution, the body inherently signifies. How the body signifies, whether descriptively or performatively, depends first on what the body signifies.

For Augustine, the erect posture of the body signifies God.[49] The body, as locus of signification, manifests God, not as something exterior to the body, nor again as something inherent to the body, but as presence. Though God is nowhere, Augustine notes, God *possesses* everything and consequently, insofar as things are, things reveal God. Furthermore, the soul reveals God in the body by its purity. Augustine clarifies that the pure soul is not contained in place but is present to the body, for the body is loosely God's place.[50] Signs inevitably reveal in the body the omnipresence of God who is in no place, yet contains all place. The embodied soul and body is within God. Augustine clarifies that

> God is not in a place, for that which is in a place is a body, but God is not a body. Therefore he is not in a place. And yet, since he is and he is not in a place, all things are in him rather than he himself being in some place, although they are not in him as if he himself were a place. For a place is in space because it is defined by the length, breadth and with characteristic of a body. God is not like this. Everything, therefore, is in him, and he is not a place.[51]

Dimensions are within God and God is beyond them. Similarly, the mind extends beyond the body. This is significant because God's presence introduces and indeed ensures the possibility of divine manifestation through signs in the body. Conversely, with the emergence of dimensions arises also divine manifestation through signs or, better yet, in possessing all things God signifies in the *becoming* of things. He writes at *Confessions*, 'And so we see the things you have made because they are, but they are because you see them. We see outwardly that they are and inwardly that they are good.'[52] All things therefore contained within the dimensions of being exhibit, in so far as they are, God's performative signification. In God (*whom*), all things signify becoming (*what*). Creation is the (ongoing) manifesting outcome of God's performative signification. Dimensions are, conversely, the receptacle of corporeal signifying redemption in the church.

Redemption is inherent to God's performative signification of creation, which is constantly escaping the nihil of temporality. Augustine introduces a redemptive character to the signification of dimensions. He outlines the emergence of the body into temporal extension and the redemption of time in the plan of salvation. The four elements of the body correspond to the fourfold dynamic progression of dimensions into the body's solidity: 'because of the four well-known natures from which [the body] is composed – dry, wet, cold and hot – and because the movement from a point to width, from width to breadth, and from breadth to height makes for the sodality of the body.'[53] The number four is the outcome of the three movements, which together result in the body, manifesting God. Thus, one represents all things, woman and the body, two denotes the soul or humanity, three is Christ and four is God. Together, the sum of ten represents God who contains all and creation.[54] The manifestation of Christ in the body overcomes the confines of temporality. Furthermore, the emergence of corporeality from the progression of dimensions suggests signs are the constitutive origin of all things, wherein God is omnipresent, seen only as unseen. In other words, signs are performative – signs not only demonstrate God's manifestation but, in so doing, perform redemption and actualize – perhaps even produce – corporeality. Inherent to what the body signifies is where it signifies: the dimensions of the church denote the place of performative redemption.

The church, therefore, as the body of Christ, as a body tout court, signifies also. In discussing the accuracy of the dimensions of Noah's ark in the Old Testament in *City of God*, Augustine insists on the historicity of the deluge narrative and its prefiguration of the church because 'the events actually took place, they signify something beyond themselves, and what they signify pertains to prefiguring the Church'.[55] Though how the dimensions of Noah's ark prefigure the church is unclear in this passage, considered in isolation, a better sense can be acquired in light of the figure of the cross at Eph. 3.18. By way of speculative interpretation, the dimensions of the Ark are the dimensions of the cross whereby the church, safeguarded from the depth of the ocean, then saved by the depth of God's mystery of grace poured forth from the unseen part of the cross. The dimensions of the body, captured by the respective dimensions of the figure of the cross, offer the foreground to understand the signification of the cross specifically in the manifestation of the mystery of grace. The final point is that signification is not simply descriptive. Signification is performative. Since the invisible grounds everything that is visible, the visible necessarily and always performs what it signifies. Signification is the act of performative manifestation in the cross. All creation springs forth as redeemed creation, as recreation, in the cross as the paradigm of manifestation.

Performative manifestation

Operative in the exegesis of the figure of the cross at Eph. 3.18, this section shows, is a mechanism of performative signification whereby the church, as the body of Christ, visibly renders the invisible graces of Christ. Augustine's treatment of dimensions and manifestation of signs is the foothold for his simultaneously developing views on the performative signification of the figure of the cross. For Augustine, as this section shows, the figure of the cross at Eph. 3.18 effects the performative signification of the church. Augustine is interested in the denotation of the dimensions of the cross from early on. For instance, in *The Catholic Way of Life and the Manichean Way of Life*, dimensions denote, and indeed exhort, a unified life in the practice of faith, rooted in truth and wisdom, and leading to happiness.⁵⁶ There is, as of yet, no mention of the cross until a few years later. Years later, in *On Christian Doctrine*, Augustine identifies the dimensions of Eph. 3.18 with the figure of the cross and focuses on the image of the unseen part of the cross comparing it to the roots of hyssop. He cites 1 Cor. 8.1 to contrast the pride of knowledge and the proliferation of love, 'knowledge puffs up, love builds up'. The love of Christ is the Passover sacrifice at 1 Cor. 5.7.⁵⁷ The sign on the door with hyssop, marked with the blood of the sacrificial lamb, and then on the people of Israel, is the lens Augustine adopts to interpret the dimensions of the cross at Eph. 3.18. The hyssop 'is a humble and gentle herb, and there is nothing stronger or more penetrating than its roots – so that rooted and founded in love, we may be able to comprehend with all the saints what is the breadth and length and height and depth, that is to say, the Lord's cross'.⁵⁸ The biological metaphor of roots allows Augustine to unearth the meaning of the sign of the cross that Eph. 3.18 denotes. Love is rooted in the depth of the cross and flourishes thereafter as an antidote to the pride of knowledge. Love is therefore sacrificial and is foretold as an antidote, that is, a performative sign, in the manifestation of the sing of the cross. What does the cross signify? Augustine explains:

> Its breadth refers to the cross-beam, where his hands are stretched out; its length to the part of the; ground as far as this breath, where his whole body from the arms down is fixed; its height to the part from the breath upwards to the top, where his head is, while the depth is what is hidden by being fixed in the ground. The sign of the cross encompasses the whole of Christian activity: doing good works in Christ and persevering in adhering to him; hoping for heavenly things, not profaning the sacraments. Purified by this kind of activity, we shall have the capacity to know also the love of Christ which surpasses all knowledge.⁵⁹

The purification of the cross by the medicinal metaphor of the sacrifice of the cross in the anointing of hyssop offers access to the humble knowledge of God's fullness in Christ, as per Eph. 3.19. While the dimensions of the cross are identified, the interpretation centres around the manifestation of the fullness of God in Christ. Eventually, Augustine returns to the image of roots which denote grace as the foundation for good works.⁶⁰ The grace of Christ is the hidden part of the tree which inevitably is expressed in good works. Furthermore, the rooting in the charity of Christ is embedded within a communal and ecclesial framework, the land of the living. Without grace, there is no continuity with the manifestation of good works, and conversely, good works always imply the unseen roots in grace. The roots of hyssop and its fragrance symbolize the invisible part of the cross and its healing effects. At play is the dynamism of signifying manifestation of God's power on the cross in the visible distribution of graces in the unseen remedial roots of the cross. Augustine emphasizes the unseen depths of grace. Upon reading Paul, Augustine identifies the unseen, hidden part of the cross, the dimension of depth, with the mysterious source of God's invisible grace. The attention later shifts to questions of grace and divine dispensation thereof. To appreciate the distribution of grace, Augustine exhorts being rooted and grounded in charity: 'For in this passage it was not the saints that the Apostle prohibited from seeking to learn but rather those who are not yet rooted and grounded in charity so as to be able to grasp with all the saints the breadth, length, height and depth and the other things that speaks of in the same place.'⁶¹ The unseen roots of charity condition understanding of the divine mysteries of grace and (eventually also) predestination. The cross therefore mediates the manifestation of (in)visible grace, the mystery of God on the cross.

The cross functions also as a performative sign. Augustine develops the pouring forth of grace from its unseen depths. He explains the extension of the cross in terms of Eph. 3.18 and with the question of the merit of grace in the foreground. Rest is the reward of good works, and it inspires labouring with joy: 'Rejoice in hope' (Rom. 12.12). He turns to the cross.

> The breadth of the cross in the transverse beam, to which the hands are nailed, symbolize this joy. For we understand the works in the hands and the joy of the worker in the breadth, because sadness causes narrowness. In height of the cross, which the head touches, we understand the expectation of rewards from the lofty justice of God [Rom. 2.6-7]. Therefore, the length of the cross, by which those who are patient are called long-suffering. But the depth of the cross, which is inserted into the

earth, symbolizes the secret of the mystery [Eph. 3.17-18]. But those things that we do not yet see and do not yet possess are symbolized by the other two days. Those things, after all, that we now do when we have been fastened as if by the nails of the commandments to the fear of God [Ps. 119.120] are counted among what is necessary; they are not among those things that are to be sought and desired for their own sake. For this reason he says that he desires that greatest good [Phil. 1.23-4]. From this moment there begins the rest that is not interrupted, but glorified by the resurrection. It is, nonetheless, not possessed by faith [Heb. 2.4]. For it is not yet been carried to fulfillment in us who are still groaning in ourselves and awaiting the adoption, the redemption of our body. (Rom. 8.23)[62]

The dimensions of the cross embed good works within the suffering of Christ and the temporal redemption rooted in faith and accessible in the hope of faith. The groaning body – a figure of the *totus Christus*, the church – is rooted in the unseen part of the cross, awaiting redemption on the agony of the cross by following the commands. The figure of the cross is not only symbolic. The figure of Christ imitating the figure of the cross is the source whereby grace is poured forth from the invisible depths of the cross. The suffering of Christ is, by implication, performative and dependent on the figure of the cross. That is, the figure of the cross on the body of Christ functions as a performative sign of divine manifestation. The form of the cross inherently manifests visibly the invisible God in Christ. The figure of the cross conveys the invisible reality signified by its depth. Grace is therefore efficacious or performative and not simply descriptive, that is, in signifying grace, the figure of the cross is *doing* something. What, then, does the figure of the cross *do*?

Augustine comes to the full appreciation of the figure of the cross soon after the sacking of Rome by Alaric. In the year 411, Augustine identifies the dimensions of God's mystery are those of the cross.

> In this mystery the shape of the cross is revealed. For he who died because he willed it died as he willed. Not in vain, then, did he choose this kind of death, but in order that in it he might also be seen as the teacher of this breadth, length, height, and depth. For the breadth is in that wood that is fixed above as a crossbeam; the length is found in that piece that is visible from this beam to

the earth; for on it one stands, that is, persists and perseveres, which is something we attribute to long-suffering. The height is seen in that part of the wood that is left to rise upward form the crossbeam; this is at the head of the crucified because the expectation of those with good hope is on high. But that part of the wood which is not seen, which is fixed and hidden and from which the whole rises, signifies the depth of gratuitous grace, in which the minds of many are exhausted when they tried to investigate it. (Rom. 9.20)[63]

The cross captures the wisdom and love of God in the unseen part of the cross, knowable only through the manifestation of its other parts. Dimensions encompass the bounds of community and converge in the mystery of the depths of the cross. For this reason, Augustine notes that the mystery of Christ's grace springs forth from the buried foot of the cross, for 'the mystery of the figure of the cross is shown in this'.[64] This is a deeply sacramental exposition of Eph. 3.18. The shape of the cross therefore expresses the mystery of grace. Before developing the sacramental performativity of the cross in the making of *community* and *Church*, what is at play in the dynamism of (in)visibility and God's manifestation?

The performative dynamics of the cross arise from the bridge of (in)visibility by means of love. God's manifestation in Christ articulates the dynamism of invisibility. The central question is how to reconcile divine epiphanies and the statement, 'no one has ever seen God'? (Jn 1.18). Augustine begins by identifying the vision of God with the Son in the Old Testament. God is, in a sense, manifest yet hidden in Christ. Then Augustine distinguishes between corporeal vision and spiritual vision. Christ is seen, even by the apostles, with the body but not recognized with the spirit. Christ is visible only when the spirit is pure, when the heart is pure (Matt. 5.8). The locus of the vision of God is not a place but the heart. The purity of heart is not based on either an innate faculty or the merited capacity of recognition. Augustine stresses the dependence on grace which is needed to see God, even after the resurrection. Finally, the great paradox of divine presence and in-visibility is formulated in this: 'When we believe [God] absent, we see him; and when he is present, we don't see him.'[65] This paradox illustrates why the apostles, though they lived with Christ, were not able to recognize him.[66] At this point Augustine inserts Eph. 3.18 to describe the omnipresence of Christ through charity. The dimensions of the cross constitute the architecture of charity denoted in its 'length and width and height and depth'.[67] To see the charity of Christ, represented by the dimensions of the cross, is to see Christ and also to see God. Though indirectly, God can be seen through the charity of Christ which is recognized as a gift of grace mediated by the figure of the cross. Community, specifically the church, embeds divine manifestation.

The performative dimension of the depths of the figure of the cross is heightened where the depths of grace is the source of community. The love of common life is antidote to the private pride that festers within. Christ dwells in the heart by means of love in good works.

> Hence love itself is now practiced in good works of charity, by which it stretches itself out to help in whatever way it can, and this is its breadth. Now it endures adversity with magnanimity and perseveres in sake of obtaining the eternal life that is promised to it on high, and this its height. But this love, on which we are in a sense founded and rooted, comes from a hidden source. There we do not search out the reasons of God's will [Rom. 11.33-35]. And this is the depth. *Altitudo* is, of course, a term common to what is high and what is deep. When, however, it is used in the sense of high, it emphasizes the eminence of loftiness, but when it is used in the sense of deep, it emphasizes the difficulty of investigation and knowledge.[68]

The depth denotes the hidden reasons of God's grace at Rom. 11.33: 'they have hidden reasons, for, since there are no preceding merits, what do we have that we have not received?'[69] The life of the heart in Christ ensures a life 'for age upon age, from the beginning of faith up to the end, which is vision'.[70] What results is an exemplary community: 'This is the communion of a divine and heavenly commonwealth; from it the poor are satisfied, not seeing the things that are their own, but those of Jesus Christ, that is, not pursuing private advantages, but looking out for what is common, in which is found the well being of all.'[71] Augustine summarizes,

> To comprehend what, then? He says: *what is the breadth* in good works, as I already said, by which good will is stretched out even to the love of enemies, and *length* in order that we may with longaminity endure sufferings on behalf o this breadth,

and *height* in order that, in return for this, we may hope for an eternal reward above, not something vain and temporal, and *depth* from which the grace of God comes gratuitously according of the secret and hidden plan of his will.[72]

The comprehension of the fullness of God is manifested in the mystery of the cross as community, precisely as church. Years later, the community is explicitly the church, and the grace of the cross ensures its unity across the world, rooted in grace, as exemplified by the seamless tunic of Christ. Dimensions of the tunic imply the unity of the church across the world in charity. The *tractatus* begins by stating the aim: to explain what happened by the cross as Christ the Saviour hung on it. Augustine comparatively analyses the drawing lots by the soldiers of Christ's seamless tunic. The narrative at Jn 19.23-24 is the most detailed as compared to Matt. 27.35, Mk 15.34 and Lk. 23.34. The tunic at the foot of the cross serves as a metaphor for the church and Christ. The division of the clothes of Christ signifies the figure of the church divided with balance in the four parts of the world. In contrast to the division, the seamless tunic played represents the unity of all these parts by the links of charity. Charity is the link of perfection (Col. 3.14) surpassing all knowledge (Eph. 3.19). Charity is seamless and can never be undone, from above to below, made of a single tissue because the Christians are united (*Io. eu. tr.* 118.4). The separation of the clothes, in spite of unity, represents the division of grace among the elected. The unity is intimately weaved into the recognition of the identity of Christ by all. When asking about the identity of Christ, as Son of God, only Peter responds.[73] The question is, for Augustine, addressed to the whole and responded to by Peter for the whole. Finally, the lot is the grace of God (*Dei gratia*) which is shared agreeably among all. Augustine contrasts the unity of the tunic and the division of the clothes: the tunic is lost to all in one, so too the grace is spread among all because all are one. While the seamless tunic allows Augustine to frame the question of grace and election at a community level where unity and division are joined, the question of the secret judgement of God in spreading grace and election with regard to merits remains unanswered. The question is no longer about the reception of grace because in unity it reaches all but about the distribution. The distribution is based on neither person nor merit but on the secret judgement of God. Whereas some followed Christ, some persecuted

Christ. The followers, discussed by the tunic, are now contrasted to the persecutors, who crucify Christ. Augustine thus introduces the image of the cross which was made and to which Christ was thrust by enemies. The image of the cross functions to reinforce the aspects of the seamless tunic: division, unity. Ultimately, the members are also crucified on the cross with Christ. The cross demonstrates grace in the unity of the church, yet the figure of the cross also makes grace in the becoming of church.[74] The body of Christ on the cross extends beyond the physical confines of its dimensions to signify the performativity of the church, that is, the body of Christ. This is why Augustine insists on the continuity of bodies, as Daniel Cardó[75] has rightly noted: the real (not simply metaphorical) continuity between the body on the cross and the body of the Eucharist: 'We too are fed from the Lord's Cross . . . when [*quia*, that is, because] we eat his body.'[76] Partaking in this extended continuity, the believer enjoins its body to the body of Christ on the cross and in the process becomes church. Augustine continues elsewhere,

> The bread which you can see on the altar, sanctified by the word of God, is the body of Christ. That cup, or rather what the cup contains, sanctified by the word of God, is the blood of Christ. [. . .] If you receive them well, you are yourselves what you receive. The Apostle therefore says: *For we, being many, are one bread, one body.* (1 Cor. 10.17) (Emphasis in original)[77]

Consuming the body of Christ on the altar fully implements the effects of the cross and constitutes the performative identification of the believer to Christ and to others in the church, as evidenced in the words, 'therefore receive and eat the body of Christ, yes, you that have become members of Christ in the body of Christ; receive and drink the blood of Christ. In order not to be scattered and separated, eat what binds you together.'[78] The remembrance of Christ actively binds those who partake in the Eucharist, and, in so doing, the graces of Christ conferred from the cross are visibly manifested on the altar. Augustine continues,

> When his body, remember, was pierced by the lance, it poured forth the water and the blood by which he cancelled our sins. Be mindful of this grace as you work out your salvation, since it is God who is at work in you, and approach with fear and

trembling to partake of this altar. Recognize in the bread what hung on the cross, and in the cup what flowed from his side.[79]

The cross visibly manifests in the making of church, the invisible graces it confers. The church is the outcome of the performative signification of the figure of the cross. Hence, the statement 'from the depth which you cannot see rises everything that you can see'[80] implies that the invisible is the origin of all things visible. Furthermore, this process of emergence, from invisibility to manifestation, is generative, thus suggesting that Augustine embraces a performative view of the church. Performativity manifests the church. The invisibility of absence, according to this model, does not affect belonging.

Conclusion

Losing faith in the power of the invisible due to the destructive consequences of an invisible pathogen has resulted, unfortunately, in discarding the invisibility of presence from a distance as a central aspect of belonging. This is physical distance, in terms of the diffused church, but also a temporal distance, in terms of the death of the cross and its ongoing work of salvation. Consequently, visibility is conflated with belonging, and the aching cry for presence and solidarity loses sight of the powerful depths of invisibility. However, invisibility is central to belonging for Augustine. This is not simply a physical distance. It is distance of perception. The invisible roots all reality. Only in recognizing this is the world redeemed by the performative manifestation of belonging. In an itinerary towards deconfinement, therefore, the purification of sight is necessary. We must learn to unsee the visible anew and in so doing shall we dwell anew. From the agony of Christ on the cross, the head of the Whole Christ, arises all the church, wherever it may be, diffused throughout the earth. Invisibility, therefore, grounds the visible manifestation of church and belonging. Thus, 'from the depth which you cannot see rises everything that you can see'.[81] The invisible community, at a distance, demands a reconsideration of belonging primarily as manifestation and becoming. Belonging is a labour of radiating, even in the absence of a community, that though diffused throughout the earth, the distressed body of Christ remains one in Christ. What does belonging at a distance, in the passage from invisibility to manifestation, make of our times? To see anew demands the retrieval of time lost during the confinement. What, in other words, is being redeemed in the manifesting process of belonging from the cross? What is the fruit of belonging's making?

5

The metamorphosis of belonging

Virgil wrote, 'Irretrievable time is flying'.[1] This proverbial phrase captures the disorienting and scattering experience produced by confinement this past year. As the pandemic ends, the retrieval of time lost during confinement arises as the most pressing requirement for any itinerary towards progressive de-confinement. What do we make of time in confinement, has it been wasted and what demands do retrieving 'lost time' pose for belonging anew? Thus arises the question, from whence does time flow, wherein does time vanish, and is the flight of time irretrievable? The question of the retrieval of time converges for Augustine with the restoration of finitude through God's eternity. Therefore, the search for and the restoration of lost time are essential requirements of a post-pandemic itinerary of de-con-finement, spiritual and material.[2] How can de-confinement – the unmaking and remaking of confines within the matrix of the fabric of finitude, that is, the metamorphosis of finitude, which Emmanuel Falque describes as 'the possibility of the impossible'[3] – re-cover and re-store the passing of lost time? The search for lost time is not about retrieving the irretrievable or simply about recollecting time, nor is it about imposing meaning upon the experience of desolation. To recover time is to deal with the *restlessness* (Augustine) and *dread* (Heidegger) caused by the unfolding of impossible possibilities left behind by the constraints of confinement. Recovering time is about transformative retrieval, about death and rebirth in the face of the inevitable, and about recognizing the *metamorphosis of finitude* at the juncture of time and eternity. Metamorphosing retrieval flows in the midst of incarnate dwelling by learning to see anew. Belonging is thus primarily not about distance or presence but fundamentally about perception. Belonging acquires a transformative sense when we perceive all things anew, from the eternal vantage point of God. In closing *Confessions*, Augustine writes, 'And so we see the things you have made because they are, but they are because you see them.'[4] The eternal presence of God's gaze conditions all existence. The retrieval of lost time consists of reconfiguring finitude and the passing of time through the unifying and creative divine gaze. To belong is to gaze just as we are gazed upon from the vantage point of eternity. Only then do all things become new.

In search of lost time

Augustine echoes a similar sentiment when he writes,

> but for now my years are wasted with sighing, and you are my comfort, O Lord; you are my eternal Father. But I am scattered through times whose order I do not know, and my thoughts, the inmost entrails of my soul, are torn to shreds by turbulent changes, until the time comes when I flow into you, purified and melted by the fire of your love.[5]

Three models may frame the relation between time and eternity. These are rooted in the Gospel of John.[6] The Greek reads, 'Καὶ ὁ λόγος σὰρξ ἐγένετο.' And the Latin is, 'et Verbum caro factum est.' The models emphasize, first, *the* Word (λόγος) and second, *the* flesh (σάρξ). Thus, in response to frames 'form above' emphasizing disincarnate Word or Spirit – for instance, in German idealism – Falque adopts finitude and corporeality as a standpoint 'from below',[7] to navigate the rift from 'time to eternity'.[8] This approach is not to be confused with the finite – finitude and the finite are not the same – or, again, with carnal hermeneutics – corporeal and carnal are not the same – which seeks 'the surplus of meaning arising from our carnal embodiment, its role in our experience and understanding, and its engagement with the wider world. [. . .] Word *is* flesh.'[9] Falque's hermeneutics is neither only of the spirit (λόγος), nor only of the flesh (σάρξ), but of the incarnation where spirit and flesh meet in finitude. Falque thus inverses the directionality of Heidegger's method. The German philosopher writes in *The Concept of Time*: 'a question of this kind – from eternity to time – is justified only on condition that we know what eternity is and that we have a sufficient understanding of it.'[10] Since we know eternity insufficiently, Heidegger discards it as the point of departure. However, though the temporal is indeed the point of departure, this does not mean the eternal remains inaccessible. On the contrary, to recognize, as does Augustine, that all things visible pour forth from what is invisible is also to recognize the transformative and indeed metamorphosing power of the resurrection, even on time. Because of the resurrection, in time and 'from below' lies the promise of eternity. Falque postulates the metamorphosis of the resurrection as the foundation of finitude, where the flesh is born anew in the body. He writes, 'The resurrection, cornerstone of Christianity, is ontologically the first principle of everything or, better, of the whole, including the creation itself projected by God.'[11] Falque attempts to insert eternity within an immanent frame of experience. But what if the resurrection is *not* the first metamorphosis? The genesis of time, the emanation of creation and indeed the incarnation itself are all *ontologically* prior to the resurrection – even as the resurrection may be the proper *epistemological* lens to understand them, but only derivatively. Eternity *must be* the starting point of experience to understand the *be-coming* and *re-covering* of time. Falque does not believe that Spinoza's view applies today (*Sub specie aeternitatis*).[12] However, Falque's view relies on a bifurcation of time and eternity, foreign to Augustine. Augustine believes that though eternity is in the human heart, the mind cannot comprehend divine time (Ecc. 3.11). The stillness of eternity is in the midst of the mundane, the ordinary, in the flow of time. The beginning is not for Augustine, as Falque argues, a punctual genesis of time (following Aquinas and), in contrast to the incarnation (Irenaeus) and the resurrection (Bonhoeffer).[13] For Augustine, every instant distension is an incarnate, transformational beginning, an ever-present glimpse of (re)creation, of metamorphosis and a manifestation of eternity in the fabric of finitude. Taking Falque a step further, therefore, the hypothesis we advance is that for Augustine, time is the *metamorphosis of eternity*. Time bears the vestiges of eternity. Eternity, inherent and indeed constitutive of time, and not external to time, is therefore *the* point of departure to retrieve, recollect and redeem (lost) time. Time construed as the *metamorphosis of eternity* alone offers the framework to begin a retrieval of lost time.

Augustine's conceptual foreground for *a-temporal* retrieval requires unearthing the paradoxical relation between time and eternity.[14] Falque explains, 'Theological eternity, whether it is "a-temporal" (above time and including all time) or "intemporal" (an indefinite continuum of successive moments), should therefore be a direct consideration of time starting from time itself, and not the converse – not the view that only an "outside-time" can legitimate time.'[15] Thus, arises the question, how can eternity (intemporal or a-temporal) relate to time? Hitherto, the learned literature has articulated various approaches found in Augustine's thought to bridge time and eternity. Some are 'from below' (beginning with time), and others are 'from above' (beginning with eternity). These have been studied from varied angles including signification,[16] a sensualist analysis of time,[17] a method of apophatic theology or the *via negativa*,[18] the manifestation of God or theophany,[19] the gradual ascent of the soul in ecstasy,[20] the interplay of grace and merit in free will and divine foreknowledge,[21] the overcoming temporality,[22] a constricted psychological experience of time,[23] the implications of time on moral philosophy,[24] the metaphysical unfolding of time within eternity[25] and a complex twofold approach to objective/subjective time.[26] Overall, these attempts to reconcile time and eternity – all with great merit – rely on a conceptual framework where time is ever at odds and even in contradiction with eternity. Reflections usually adopt one of the following as a point of departure: either time ('from below'), that is, a model of the flesh (σάρξ), or eternity ('from above'), that is, a model of the Word (λόγος). There remains a third, yet unexplored *via* ('from between' or the μεταξύ), wherein time and eternity are manifested as *transformative becoming* (ἐγένετο) in the incarnation. Plotinus identifies the path 'from between' as the rightful place of humanity, somewhere between divinity and animals: 'But humanity, in reality, is poised midway between gods and beasts, and inclines now to the one order, now to the other; some men grow like to the divine, others to the brute, the greater number stand neutral.'[27] However, traversing the path 'from between' is ever assailed by the human illusion of self-sufficiency and the consequence of hubris, following the words in John: 'For all that is in the world – the lust of the flesh, the lust of the eyes, and worldly ambition – is not of the Father but is of the world.'[28] The only antidote to human frailty is therefore the incarnation. God must reveal humanity a model to follow and an ideal of what it means to be human in Christ. Thus, the model 'from between' is the framework of embodiment, where Word and flesh morph. This study presents music as the paradigm of the *via* 'from between', the model of *metamorphosing* unity and manifestation of Word and flesh in the ebb of time and eternity.

Puzzling at the mystery of life's passing, Augustine writes in *Confessions*, 'what shall I call it? – this life that dies, this death that lives? I do not know.'[29] If all is transitory, and if life is truly a process of becoming, can there be a point of departure 'from between' and can there be a point of departure at all? The point of departure is love. This is what Augustine comes to learn, following Paul who writes,

> If I speak in the tongues of men and of angels, but have not love, I am a noisy gong or a clanging cymbal. And if I have prophetic powers, and understand all mysteries and all knowledge, and if I have all faith, so as to remove mountains, but have not love, I am nothing. If I give away all I have, and if I deliver up my body to be burned, but have not love, I gain nothing. Love is patient and kind; love does not envy or boast; it is not arrogant or rude. It does not insist on its own way; it is not irritable or resentful; it does not rejoice at wrongdoing, but rejoices with the truth. Love bears all things, believes all things, hopes all things, endures all things. Love never ends.[30]

Love is thus a vestige of eternity. But love, too, like all else, is immersed in the river of time. Augustine explores the aporias of moving towards the unknowable and forgotten memory of God, inevitably and always frustrated by the dissipation of time: 'Late have I loved you, beauty so ancient and so new! Late have I loved you! And behold, you were within, but I was outside and looked for you there, and in my ugliness I seized upon these beautiful things that you have made. You were with me, but I was not with you.'[31] The inescapable belatedness of love surfaces in the paradoxes of time. Namely, how to overcome the finitude of time within time, that is, how to *de*-fine time? Augustine *de*-fines time in relation to eternity. Time is inherently a dissipation, a flux of perpetual motion. Time is broken; eternity is wholesome. Augustine presents three paradoxes of time arising from this brokenness inherent to the human condition.[32] The first paradox concerns the relationship between the temporality of creation and the eternity of God. The second is about how to measure time. Lastly, whether time exists at all, and if it does, how can time *be* at all, when by definition, time tends *to not be*. In all three cases, the paradoxes of time arise because of the complicated relationship between the motions of time and the stillness of eternity, both of which are inherent to music.

To say God is eternal means God is without beginning or end and unchanging or immutable. Although eternity is without origin, eternity is the origin of time.[33] This raises the thorny question posed by the Manicheans – and to which Augustine frequently returned – on the relation between eternity and the genesis of creation and temporality. That is, 'What was God doing before he made heaven and earth?'[34] To address this question, Augustine draws from Plotinus to articulate God's eternity and concludes, as Teske notes, that 'God does not precede time by time'.[35] For Augustine, God is immutable and unchanging, and therefore beyond time because 'what suffers no change is better than what can be changed'.[36] Augustine takes the concept of the timelessness of divine eternity from the *Enneads* of Plotinus. Plotinus writes, for instance:

> it is never other and is not a thinking or life that goes from one thing to another but is always the selfsame and without extension or interval; seeing all this one sees eternity in seeing a life that abides in the same and always has the all present to it, not now this, and then again that, but all things at once, and not now some things, and then again others, but a partless completion, as if they were all together in a point, and had not yet begun to go out and flow into lines; it is something which abides in the same in itself and does not change at all but is always in the present, because nothing of it has passed away, nor again will anything of it come into being, but that which it is, it is.[37]

God is the self-same or the *idipsum*.[38] God is therefore infinite and eternal, which is well captured a century later, by the definition of eternity in *Consolation of Philosophy*: 'Eternity is a possession of life, a possession simultaneously entire and perfect, which has no end.'[39] Although Augustine defines time in function of eternity following Plotinus, he does so with an important variant. Following the Psalms, eternity for Augustine is not only without end but also without beginning.[40] Thus, Augustine eloquently concludes of God: 'your today is your eternity.'[41] Similarly, Augustine describes God's eternity as an act of omnipresence: 'everywhere as a whole (*ubique totus*).'[42] God's substance is immutable. Predicating substance, even of God's eternity, is problematic.[43] Therefore, Marion notes, eternity as God's substance is a negative mode of God's *de*-nomination in relation to the mutability of creation.[44] Since time is a result of eternity, time must be defined in terms of eternity. Time is nowhere whole because time is dissipated eternity.

What, then, is time? Augustine puzzles over the nature of time in its relation to eternity, or better yet, in its genesis from eternity. Augustine poses the question: 'So what is time? If no one asks me, I know; if I want to explain it to someone who asks me, I do not know.'[45] The paradox of time is that, although rooted in infinite and immutable eternity, time is ephemeral. Time therefore has an escaping quality to it, as Teske notes, 'for neither past nor future time is, and present time *is* only by ceasing to be'.[46] Time is therefore 'the tendency not to be'.[47] This observation leads Augustine to echo Plato's attribution of time to the present alone in the *Timaeus*.[48] Following Plato, though not exactly, Augustine attributes existence to the present alone when he writes:

> If indeed future and past things exist, I want to know where they are. If I do not yet have the strength to know where they are, I do at least know that wherever they are, they are not future or past there, but present. For if they are future there, they do not yet exist there; and if they are past there, they no longer exist there. So wherever they are, whatever they are, they must be present.[49]

Thus, he offers the first of two definitions of time: 'It is now clear and evident that neither future things nor past things exist. Nor is it strictly correct to say, "There are three times: past, present, and future." Instead, it would perhaps be correct to say, "There are three times: the present of things past, the present of things present, and the present of things future."'[50] All times are related to the present. And if time is present, the instant moment of time does not truly exist, aside from a duration – and again, is this a mode of existence? The duration of the present is to time what a dot is to a line, that is, time is definable only in relation to duration. Time is relational duration, therefore.[51] Since the duration of time *is* only in *relation* to the soul, Augustine identifies the soul as the yardstick to measure time.[52] Augustine writes, 'I see, therefore, that time is a kind of distention (*distentio*).'⁵³ Complimentary to this first passive disposition, Augustine also defines time as an active straining forward and oriented towards the future: 'straining forward in intention'.⁵⁴ Time is therefore eternity extended, eternity *with* duration – eternity *de*-nominated? The *relationality* of time is dynamic, metamorphosing and always productive in becoming. Thus arises the central hypothesis of the present study, that is, stillness of time (in music) manifests the metamorphosis of eternity 'from between', as per the model of incarnation, in and as becoming. The incarnation as union of Word and flesh retrieves the dissipation of time by the death of Christ on the cross – the *death of death*⁵⁵ – and the resurrection. This *death of death* constitutes a metamorphosis of eternity whereby 'every person is objectively lifted up to the changeless years of eternity'.⁵⁶ Accordingly, Christ's *death of death* is the condition for the unfolding of the *metamorphosis of finitude*, the impossible possibility. With the *metamorphosis of finitude* operative in the foreground, the *making* of music within time, its performance, emerges. The motions of music, like those of time, frame Augustine's understanding of time as the metamorphosis of eternity.

The music of time

Augustine notes that God utters the eternal Word all at once in the flesh of the incarnation.⁵⁷ The analogy of music and language is helpful to articulate this metamorphosing unfolding of eternity in the midst of time. The performance of music is the paradigmatic model of the incarnation, and therefore, music's constant rhythms temporarily reflect the immutability of eternity.⁵⁸ Thus the performance of music offers an approach to bridging time and eternity whereby the eternal of music transforms reality and broken time. The central question for Augustine, with regard to the temporality of music, is as follows: What does music *do*? The belatedness of delight, it was noted earlier, reveals the question of time inherent to music. Like the incarnation, music *orders* and *possesses* temporality by means of rhythms. For this reason, Augustine was intrigued by the paradoxical *doing* of music, at once precipitous and gradual: '"the precipitous grasping at the contemplation of blessedness" and the gradual step by step way (of understanding) determined by music's own "possessions and order".'⁵⁹ The mechanics of language afford Augustine a framework to understand the paradoxical relation between the gradual unfolding of 'possession and order' and the resulting, punctual moment of contemplation. That is, music, like the incarnation, offers an image of the eternal (punctual contemplation) and the temporal (gradual ascent). The dynamic reveals music is a kind of language. In fact, Lombardi rightly insists, for Augustine, 'time *is* language'.[60] Music thereby functions as the grammar of time.[61] Much like language, music (which is really but a special manoeuvring of language) becomes intelligible only in the process of extension or duration, from a letter into a syllable, and from a syllable into a word and finally as a sentence. A sentence becomes meaningful only in the retrospective understanding of what is in memory, in a single moment of recollection. Conversely, single letters in language are void of extension and length. They are simple and punctual and remain void of meaning. Why? Because they do not signify anything as of yet. The meaning of music, like that of language, lies in its ability to function as signs and in so doing to signify. Augustine considered words as signs and recognized that in music, words delayed by rhythm and pace run the risk of thwarting their signification. Sound may therefore sever a sound from its sign, as Augustine rightly notes.[62] Accordingly, the problem of music emerges as a special case of the problem of signification and the ability of the sounds of words to convey rightly, what they signify in a specific formatting according to the laws of music.

What are these laws? Music is governed by rhythms, and rhythms are produced by giving number and length to the motions of time – a combination of rhythms sequentially arranged from the basic units for ensuring continuity. This is what Augustine calls a 'continuous rhythm'.[63] Since continuity determines the possibility of rhythms, rhythms must be identified with the continuity of the present as 'the present of the present'.[64] What does this mean? To explain, by analogy, rhythm is to word what a continuous rhythm is to a sentence. Words are the basic units governing the possibility of signification in language, but meaning in a sentence is only obtained by sequential ordering or numbering in length in the continuous rhythms. Augustine unsurprisingly attaches much interest to the connectives warranting measure continuity of motion. The most basic musical unit containing a dose of meaning is the verse (*versus*),[65] where the totality of a set of units obtains parallelism in the midst of various divisions. Music conveys meaning in beauty by means of a concordance, defined as undisturbed 'balance of temporal units'.[66] The possibility of music relies on following the laws which govern the manipulation of rhythms to produce continuous rhythms. These, in turn, when harmonize, produce a concordance analogous to the meaning that a sentence also produces. The application of a grammar of music is useful to frame the mechanics of music and its relation to time.

Does a purely grammatical derivation of signification, through a progressive construction of meaning, from simple units into a complex holistic system of meaning, satisfactorily explain the simultaneous punctuality and extension of music? The answer is no. Music functions like language because it is language, the grammar of time. Thus, in a sense music does signify. However, it also has its peculiarities. In identifying the peculiarities of music, the problem of how music signifies different from regular, non-musical language comes to the fore. As mentioned previously, in the absence of rhythm, sounds often run the risk of thwarting the connection or coupling between sounds and what they signify. This is because music not only describes reality by means of words but also affects reality by enlivening material.[67] Music is therefore not only descriptive but most importantly, performative.[68] Music *does* something, and it is creative. Following Austin's influential definition, the aim of a *performative utterance*, in the case of music a rhythmic sound, 'is not to describe my doing of what I should be said in so uttering to be doing or to state that I am doing it: it is to do it'.[69] Therein lies the core of music construed as the grammar of time. Music not only captures and conveys reality; in the process, music also shapes reality, transforms reality and metamorphoses reality. This gives a new perspective into the conditions for signification according to the grammar of music. Signification is (also) production – this echoes Augustine's line about wanting to make truth in *Confessions*.[70] The ability of music to signify in performative manifestation is the grounds for the metamorphosis of reality.

What and how does the performance of music produce? A direct implication of construing music in terms of production is that perhaps the single greatest difference between grammar and music is the horizon of possibilities. Music is not restricted, like grammar, in its modality of expression. The modality of music, meaning its *modus*, has a greater range of variety (quality) and number (quantity) of sounds than does language. Language is restricted by *what is* (the necessary), whereas music is determined by what *can become* (the possible). This is especially important with regard to music's ability to bridge the necessity of finitude with the innumerable possibilities for its reconfiguration, that is, its metamorphosis. Motion is an apt symbol of the transformational power of music. Augustine thus speaks of music in terms of motion and its mechanics. The motion of music is governed by basic units of pulse or strokes (*pulsus*) ordered into rational motion.[71] Within the horizon of possibility, the congruent motion of pulses effectuates the production of pleasure or voluptuousness. Thus, the delight of eloquence in music renders motions all the more rational: 'what is sweeter is clearer.'[72] Accordingly, music produces the sweetness of motions. This is significant because delight is the locus where complexity and simplicity come into contact in memory and because delight is the driving force of the metamorphosis of time. By way of anticipation and foundational explanation, to appreciate how the metamorphosis of time enters the discussion, it is necessary to first understand why Augustine had difficulty making sense of the doings of delight vis-à-vis the eternity of God Music effectuates the genesis of time through the metamorphosis of eternity, and this metamorphosis offers a framework to conceive the redemption of time, following the model of incarnation, 'from between'.

Eternity now

Music, in a special way, is able to transform time. This is because music is a prototype of how temporal creation relates to the eternal creator, God. Music is a symbol of creation, because, as mentioned before, music shapes reality in delight. Augustine discusses the beginning of creation in Genesis, the 'in the beginning' (*in principio*).[73] What does it mean that God *makes*? Augustine writes,

> But those who understand 'In the beginning God made' as meaning 'God first made' cannot offer a truthful interpretation of 'heaven and earth' unless they understand it as meaning the matter of heaven and earth, that is, the matter of the whole creation, both intelligible and bodily. For if they interpret 'heaven and earth' as meaning the whole creation as already formed, one could rightly

ask them, 'If God first made the whole creation, what did he make after that?' They will find nothing that could have been made after the whole of creation, and so they will be mortified when they hear us ask, 'How was that first if there was nothing afterward?'[74]

Augustine here focuses on the question of temporal sequence, precedence and procession. How is there a before and an after when God creates if God is not subjected to time and if God does not operate in time? To answer the question, Augustine introduces the notions of formed matter and unformed matter in order to better analyse origins ('in the beginning' in Gen. 1.1) and the nature of (temporal) precedence. Central to this is the concept of unformed matter (*material informis*).[75] Everything in creation has form and matter. Prior to acquiring a form, matter exists without a form as unformed matter. Unformed matter is, for Augustine, a non-temporal created principle of limitation.[76] Unformed matter is not subject to time, for it is without form.[77] Furthermore, form is not prior to matter, as these are co-created.[78] Thus, as matter emerges with form, it simultaneously enters the ebb of temporality. Augustine describes unformed matter as 'almost nothing' (*prope nihil*)[79] in the context of discussing the darkness prior to creation, narrated in Book XII of *Confessions*. Augustine argues the darkness is simply the absence of creation, like darkness the absence of light and silence the absence of sound. This absence is what Augustine calls 'unformed matter':[80]

> And so there was darkness over the abyss because there was no light over it, just as there is silence wherever there is no sound. For there to be silence somewhere is simply for there to be no sound there, nothing more. Have not you, O Lord, taught this soul what it confesses to you? Have not you, O Lord, taught me that before you formed this unformed matter and fashioned it into distinct things, it was not anything: not color, not shape, not body, not spirit? Yet it was not altogether nothing: it was an undifferentiated something without any form.[81]

Unformed matter is fashionable. It is not nothing, but it is not something either. Unformed matter is simply an 'undifferentiated something without a form'. Thus, *before* creation, the void and darkness represent unchanging, formless, timeless 'unformed matter' and creation is the process whereby God ascribes forms and, in so doing, the differentiation of matter emerges and enters time, with a form.

The process of creation as the shaping formless matter applies to the making of music. Silence is the unformed matter of sound and music is silence with a form. Silence only enters temporality upon receiving the shape of rhythm. Accordingly, silence is not, for Augustine, the absence of sound, or simply nothing. In early years, Augustine had difficulty understanding 'unformed matter' and would think of it as either something without form or merely as something deformed. Eventually, Augustine would conclude that 'unformed matter' is an intermediate between nothing and something. He writes, 'For I would more readily think that what was deprived of all form did not exist at all, rather than conceiving something intermediate between form and nothing, neither formed nor nothing, something unformed and nearly nothing.'[82] God creates all from unformed matter: 'For you, O Lord, made the world from unformed matter, and you made this unformed matter, which was so nearly nothing, from nothing. From unformed matter you made the great things that the children of men behold in wonder.'[83] The passage is particularly significant as it suggests silence is unformed matter, not simply the absence of sound. In other words, silence – a kind of stillness – is not nothing, yet it is not quite something. Silence is the 'unformed matter' of music, an intermediate between the motions of sound and nothingness. Silence is the stillness of eternity.

Silence is thus inherent to making music. Per-forming music consists in forming or shaping silence into sound. To form unformed silence according to rhythms is to transform the stillness of matter and to make music. This is important because silence is without time, and yet with the making of music, the rhythms of silence, time enters creation. Thus, silence lacks time, and it is a vestige in time of the stillness of eternity's beginning. Augustine writes,

> I find two things you made that lack times, though neither is coeternal with you. One was formed in such a way that it has perfect enjoyment of your eternity and immutability, without ever ceasing its contemplation, without any space of time in which it undergoes change; though it is changeable, it does not change. The other was unformed in such a way that there was nothing in it by which it could be changed from one form to

another, whether by moving or by being at rest, and so it was not subject to time. But you did not leave this unformed, because in the Beginning, before any day, you made heaven and earth: these two things of which I have been speaking.[84]

In this passage, the stillness of silence fits the description of what lacks time, which is not also co-eternal – Christ alone is co-eternal. On the one hand, silence is changeable by means of form but does not change within the heavenly sphere or the heaven of heaven, where stillness leads to a contemplation of God's unmoved eternity. On the other hand, the stillness of silence remains unmoved and therefore unaffected by time because although it can change in form, and therefore enter temporality, it has nothing within itself to do it. An external force is required. This is the earth. 'In the beginning', silence unites heaven and earth. Augustine then concludes,

> So I understand these two things – one perfectly formed from the very beginning, the other completely unformed: the first is heaven, but the heaven of heaven, and the second is earth, but earth invisible and unorganized – and my interpretation, for now, is that because of what these two things are, there is no mention of any day when Scripture says, 'In the Beginning God made heaven and earth.'[85]

The unformed matter which is silence unites the heavens and the earth at the beginning. Music as the formation of sound constitutes the passage into temporality. It requires the capacity of time to be formed, and some external form to form it. From this vantage point, music is paradoxically constituted by the motion of silence and is inherently oriented towards the original silence of God's eternity. Thus, paradoxically, the stillness of silence is the orientation of music. Yet, no music is possible without motion. Motion is only possible because of silence. In *Confessions*, albeit in a different context, a note on motion elucidates this point: 'without variation in motions there are no times, and where there is no form, there is no variation.'[86] Music as the process of forming silence into specific kinds of sounds constitutes effectively – and this is a radical hypothesis – the institution of time. Music changes silence into orderly forms that set time into *motion*: 'For in all those things the changes of times take place because of the orderly variation of motions and forms.'[87] Thus, there are echoes, and indeed vestiges, of the stillness of eternity in time. Moreover, these echoes seem to suggest that time is the metamorphosis of eternity performed by music, at least by analogy but possibly ontologically also. Music limits time and thus gives form to God's unending eternity. Music is therefore the metamorphosis of eternity.

Considered as the metamorphosis of eternity, time carries within its veil of stillness, a power of redemption, from its very inception. The *precedence* of silence to the motion of rhythms and forms is the focal point to understand this redeeming quality of the stillness of eternity. This is well illustrated in the discussion of temporal procession 'from the beginning'. Generally, all unformed matter precedes formed matter in one of four ways. This applies also to how silence precedes sound: 'in eternity, in time, in choice, and in origin. One thing precedes another in eternity as God precedes all things; in time, as the flower precedes the fruit; in choice, as the fruit precedes the flower; in origin, as sound precedes song.'[88] God precedes all things in the beginning, and things in turn precede one another. This means that precedence is analogous. All in creation is proceeded by matter in the sequences of time before receiving a shape. Not so with sound. There is no sound before song. And so, sound cannot be shaped by or formed into song. This is furthermore complicated by the fact that sound, like life and time, inherently passes away. Silence, as unformed matter, precedes music in time and yet, in attaining a form, *becomes* inherently temporal. The shape of sound is, by analogy, a shapeless shape, or better, a shape of shapelessness. Sound approximates the emergence of time as *distention*. Thus, the extension of silence results in sound, and with extension silence engenders time. Silence is not lost in sound just as in the *becoming* of time all time remains extended in *relation* to the mind measuring instantaneously the moment that is (present), that was (past) and that will be (future). Furthermore, the passage from silence into time, that is, the genesis of sound, is an excellent paradigm to think about how God 'unchangeably makes all changeable things'.[89] Even as silence happens within the time of music, silence remains an unformed form of time. Augustine writes,

> Of these four, the first and last I mentioned are quite difficult to understand; the second and third are quite easy. It is a rare and

extraordinarily demanding insight for us to contemplate your eternity, O Lord, which unchangeably makes all changeable things and is in that way prior to them. And who has such a keen mind that he can discern without great effort how sound is prior to song, precisely because song is formed sound? Certainly it is possible for something unformed to exist, but what does not exist cannot be formed. It is in this way that matter is prior to what is made out of it. Matter is not prior in the sense that it makes the thing – on the contrary, matter is what is made into the thing – nor is it prior by some interval of time.[90]

The stillness of eternity *in* time leads to contemplation 'from between'.

The silence of music metamorphoses time to contemplate eternity. Augustine explicitly explores the analogy:

> It is not that we first produce unformed sounds without song and then afterward shape or fashion those sounds into a song, as we do with the wood out of which someone makes a chest or the silver out of which someone makes a vase. Those materials are indeed temporally prior to the forms of things that are made from them, but that is not the case with song.[91]

The silence inherent to song is not produced and yet remains the foundation for transforming sound into music.

> When someone sings, one hears his sound. He does not first produce unformed sound and then form it into a song. For whatever the first sound he makes might be, it passes away, so you will not find any part of it left for you to shape into a song by means of your musical skill. So a song depends upon its sound, for its sound is its matter, the very matter that is formed so as to be a song. And this is the sense in which, as I was saying, the matter of sound is prior to the form of a song. Sound is not prior to song in the sense that it is the power to make song: sound is not the artisan that crafts song; rather, sound is subject to the soul of the singer in virtue of the body out of which he makes sound. Nor is sound prior in time, since sound is produced simultaneously with song. Nor is it prior in choice: sound is not more important than song, since song is not just sound, but sound given a beautiful

form. It is, however, prior in origin, since song is not formed in order that there might be sound, but rather sound is formed in order that there might be song. For anyone who is capable of understanding, let this example serve to explain the sense in which the matter of things was made first, and called 'heaven and earth' because heaven and earth were made from it.[92]

Silence, the unformed matter of music, is timeless and gives rise to time through metamorphosis, through change of sound things come into being, while remaining deeply grounded in eternity:

> Matter was not made first in time, for it is the forms of things that give rise to times, whereas matter was formless; and now that there are times, matter and form are perceived simultaneously. Yet we cannot help speaking of matter as if it were temporally prior. Even so, it is the least valuable thing, since formed things are obviously better than unformed things, and it is preceded by the eternity of the Creator, who made it from nothing so that from it everything could be made.[93]

The metamorphosis of eternity into time happens via the silence of music. The becoming of eternity, in turn, redeems time unto all eternity.

Music is in a sense a *symbol of time*[94] just as time is a moving *image of eternity*.[95] Yet, considered as the metamorphosing performativity of eternity, music is the very engendering form of eternity, the genesis of time, a performative sacramentality of time. It is an image of eternity, like time, but also the redeeming power in action to produce delight, to refashion the image of time in the likeness of eternity, precisely because within time hide the vestiges of eternity. Nothing is lost, therefore, in the river of time when all time is eternally held by the metamorphosed motions of eternity. All time is redeemed by the sacrament of music and so, the search for time lost, demands a reconfiguration of finitude by the metamorphosis of the delight of music. Music makes something of the truth of reality. The eternity of music transforms the reality of finitude and in so doing redeems the brokenness of temporality. Music offers a window into eternity that unifies scattered experience and voices, if but at an instant, the eternal possession of all rhythms. Music not only redeems *some* time, but by 'redeeming *the* time',⁹⁶ music too restores all things anew. 'The poverty of human understanding so often makes for an abundance of speech, for seeking says more than finding, asking takes longer than obtaining, and the hand that knocks has more to do than the hand that is open to receive.'⁹⁷ There is no music without silence, and silence speaks in the metamorphosing power of music which recovers times and upholds all time. The condition for recovering and transforming all time is paradoxically the stillness of silence, which is God's eternity. Then alone, does the metamorphosis of eternity effect the redemption of time, making 'all things new'?⁹⁸ 'If I do not abide in him, neither can I abide in myself. But he, abiding in himself, makes all things new.'⁹⁹ The redemption of time consists in abiding within the stillness of eternity which music provides. Abiding in the paradigm of music commands a form incarnate indwelling.

Conclusion

The transformation of time, ensuing from abiding anew according to the mode of the incarnation (or *becoming* Word-flesh) raises yet again the question of time's retrieval, by way of metamorphosing de-confinement. From whence does time flow, wherein does time vanish, and is the flight of time irretrievable? Falque notes that 'the difference of times so rightly taken up in theology since St. Augustine – the time of God, "who included all the times", and the time of mankind taken as a "succession of nows" – should not make us forget the *transformation of time* that the final resurrection brings to completion.'¹⁰⁰ The second coming unveils, accordingly, 'the affective modality of the moment of transition (resurrection)'.¹⁰¹ Considered 'from below', the vantage point of the flesh, *the* time is fulfilled, and therefore retrieval of time lost achieved, only in the *final* resurrection. In contrast, considered 'from between' – no longer only 'from above' (Word) or 'from below' (flesh) – the logic of the incarnation is not a promise, the condition of all times, and remains before time, the first metamorphosis, in the *becoming* of Word in the flesh. In this unity consists the true *transformation of time*, and in it lies hidden the performative genesis of time from eternity. The redemption of time is therefore not only a new modality, as Falque argues. Rather, the redemption of time, achieved before all time and inherent within time, is the modality of *transformation*; it is the very *becoming of time*. With music, the language of the incarnation, the Word takes flesh and makes all things new. Therefore, the metamorphosis of eternity performs the redemption of time, not only as resurrection but as performative genesis, as birth, which is restoration 'from between'. Under a new gaze, time as *the metamorphosis of eternity* is the condition for rendering possible the impossible. A new orientation towards time arises 'from between' as a moral imperative. The new form of dwelling, an incarnate 'dwelling among', arises as to the mode of *becoming*, that is, of *metamorphosis* 'from between' of Word-flesh (Καὶ ὁ λόγος σὰρξ ἐγένετο). The finitude of the flesh is therefore, not the point of departure, as Falque insists. The point of departure must remain the contact of time and eternity in the metamorphosing and performative unity of flesh and Word, of which music is an image. The becoming of time, the transformative manifestation of the incarnate Word-flesh must remain the modality of indwelling and of temporal recovery. Only then is restoration of lost time achieved. For such is the predicament of the human condition, always on the way (*in via*), almost there, but not yet. The Apostle Paul fittingly exhorts the Romans (and us today) to seize redemption amidst the *metamorphosing* power of faith's hope, by which the body, in the midst of time, and by the redemptive impetus of time's incarnate becoming, is constantly *being* redeemed: 'for in this hope we were saved,' writes Paul.[102] The metamorphosis of belonging fulfils the condition of temporal retrieval, beyond de-confinement, in the practice of a salvific hope – a hope wherein time too is manifested as already redeemed, but not yet fully. After the siege of Rome in 410 by Alaric's army – a symbol of the end of a civilization, and the beginning of the fall of the mighty Roman Empire – Augustine exhorts the congregation that when all else fails, the Christian is not a victim of time but the agent of time's flare: 'The times are evil, the times are troubled, that's what people say. Let us live good lives, and the times are good. We ourselves are the times. Whatever we are like, that's what the times are like.'[103] Already in our times, we belong in the heavenly city, ever reminded of the value of tears that is our temporary home, the earthly domain. We *are* the times, in a profoundly metaphysical sense, caught in the process of a metamorphosing eternity. De-con-finement is about undoing the constraints of finitude, and in so doing, transforming them anew into the eternity from whence they flow as time. In time is the promise of eternity, and thus, the retrieval of lost time consists in daring a metamorphosis of belonging. Perhaps this is what Proust means in *In Search of Lost Time*, where he writes, 'the universe is true for us all and dissimilar to each of us'.[104]

Conclusion

'When philosophy paints its grey in grey, a shape of life has grown old, and it cannot be rejuvenated, but only recognized, by the grey in grey of philosophy; the owl of Minerva begins its flight only with the onset of dusk,'[1] wrote Hegel. Hegel's insight is that we can better grasp the orientation of life's unfolding only retrospectively because temporal distance enhances perspective. Hegel thus rejoins Augustine's spirit of retrospection and *Confession* – temporal and spiritual – whereby God is found in the belated recognition that as things fall apart, everything is inevitably bound to find its resting place in the weight of love, albeit belatedly. Submersed in finitude, we are bound to always love too little, too late. 'Things that are not fully ordered are restless; they are put in order and find rest. My weight is my love: by it I am carried wherever I am carried.'[2] In chaos lies hidden the promise of redemptive love. Thenceforth, Augustine tells us, the present is reoriented as a straining forward in the accomplishment of hope:

> so that through him I might grasp the one who also has me in his grasp, and from the fragments of days past be gathered up to follow the One, forgetting those things that are past, and not stretched out through distention but straining forward in intention to the things that lie ahead (not to future things that are but fleeting), I press on toward the prize of the upward call, where I will hear the voice of praise and gaze upon your delight, which neither comes to be nor passes away.[3]

As deconfinement begins, we ask, are the shades of the pandemic's night gathering, and can this afford retrospective perspective into an unprecedented year contending with belonging as a quarantined church, and can this night offer a glimpse of dawn and, accordingly, the conditions for an itinerary of deconfinement?

The invisibility of di-stance

What does it mean to belong as church during quarantine or, what is belonging from a distance? The recognition of the distance of interiority, construed not as physical absence but as existential fissure and therefore as ontological bifurcation or di-stance, captured by the Pauline words 'the spirit is willing, but the flesh is weak',[4] constitutes Augustine's point of departure in contending with belonging from a distance. Augustine initially attempted to frame the paradoxes of di-stance's dyadic alterity according to a Platonic ontology of image, whereby difference (and sameness) simultaneously defines identity by imitating God as the self-same One. While the concept of image aimed to integrate dyadic alterity within identity at least in theory, in practice this approach required rejecting difference to attain unity in sameness. However, how to forego the di-stance characteristic of the human predicament without foregoing what it means to be human? To be human, after all, is to be a paradox – 'a life that dies, a death that lives'[5] – and therefore to articulate human existence as a question unto itself – 'I have become a question to myself.'[6] It is not possible to overcome distance by surpassing di-stance; the fissure of human experience is not only an intellectual problem but also, and primarily, an existential one, a problem of stance, of posture, of interior fragmentation and of temporal dissipation. Human experience cannot be otherwise. Only years later, by recognizing God as One and Three, or as Trinity of persons in the unity of a divine substance, Augustine managed to reconfigure the framework of alterity in terms of triadic relation. In triadic relation, the difference is not a problem to dispose of, but an inherent structure of belonging, always in relation to someone. This important shift prompted Augustine to reconsider belonging and the longing to be of human di-stance in terms of relation, for triadic relation preserves sameness and integrates difference. Far from shunning the alterity of the body and matter, and therefore the metaphysical principle of individuation, Augustine identifies the body as the efficient sign of humanity's capacity for God. The upright posture of the human body, Augustine insists, signifies its divine orientation. This is not simply a metaphor, though perhaps initially it was for the bishop of Hippo. Augustine furthermore argues for a continuity between the body of Christ on the cross and the body of Christ as the church. In other words, the body construed as relation signifies humanity's capability for God in the performative or efficacious manifestation of the body of Christ, the church. The making of belonging is not only an intellectual problem but also the inherent demand of di-stance and thus the flourishing of human life. Augustine believes belonging occurs by enjoining human suffering to the suffering body of Christ on the cross, which is the church. Thus belonging from a physical distance, and irrespective of absence, is possible. The church is the locus of human di-stance because the church reflects and transforms the humanity of human beings. With this argument, Augustine invites shifting the focus on the problem of belonging, from a question of presence/absence, or distance/di-stance, to a question of invisibility and manifestation.

In the absence of presence, the question arises, what grounds the relationship between the invisibility of church and the manifestation of belonging in the midst of suffering? Whereas prior to the pandemic, a general indifference towards invisibility abounded, mistrust of the invisible, incited by the destructive outcomes of a pathogen known not directly but only by its effects has come to surge during the isolation of quarantine. The pendulum has vacillated from apathy for the invisible to mistrust, fear and even contempt. This emerging suspicion of the invisible has at least recovered the fundamental role of what escapes the eye in human life. For Augustine, the invisible grounds the visible. In the body of Christ on the cross, the suffering of the church converges in one voice. The cross captures the paradigm of manifestation and the dynamism of (in)visibility. Moreover, the upright figure of the cross, resembling the human body with arms outstretched, is the paradigm of reality, whereby 'from the depth which you cannot see rises everything that you can see'.[7] During the isolation of the quarantine, the depth represents the distance that reveals di-stance and therefore belonging in the church. Distance reveals accordingly the very fabric of existence, rooted in the unseen and in continuous process of manifestation. Furthermore, this ongoing process of manifestation is indicative of belonging as church in an ongoing process of metamorphosis, of reconfiguration, of longing to be, of becoming, of learning to dwell anew. In Augustine's views on belonging in the church, existential distance or di-stance, irrespective of physical separation, models and roots belonging according to the figure of the cross, where the body of Christ, diffused throughout the world, enjoins the voice of Christ wherein many become one.

'God with us' or 'God for us'?

Last year, the world patiently awaited for the fulfilment of a promise of liturgical Easter celebrations in churches, only to disappointingly realize with time, that confinement would continue for an indeterminate period as the pandemic raged on. A year of separation, death and healing brings with it the promise of a new beginning, of rebirth in the Easter of the resurrection. However, Easter 2021 is in sight, and the ringing bells of empty churches continue to echo the as-of-yet unrealized expectations of deconfinement. With Augustine, longing to be, or be-longing, construed irrespective of distance, the question is no longer 'wither is God?' – with Augustine we have discovered that in the making of belonging God has been there all along – but 'with whom is God?', as Emmanuel, 'God among us.' Belonging and longing to be as church has revealed in the course of 2020 contending approaches to what it means to be church. The church is not a place; the church is a living temple where God resides. The temple of the church refers, writes Augustine, 'not to wood and stone, but to human beings, from whom, as from living stones, God's house is being built'.[8] Solari agrees on this point. The point of dispute is the mode of God's sacramental presence in the world and, consequently, the mode of being in the world, of being, longing and becoming church. Solari writes, 'God with whom? It is not possible to confess without inconsistency that the Christian God's name is "God with us" ("Emmanuel") while denying that this God is "for us", since God dwells concretely with his people always and forever – with all his people.'[9] According to this reflection, a 'God with us'[10] is a 'God for us',[11] such that the sacramental mode of divine presence in the world restricts what is given, or better who is given ('God with us') to the place where this is given ('God with us'), namely the Eucharist. By implication, belonging in the church, too, is restricted to place. However, Augustine's understanding of belonging is broader – as is his understanding of sacrament – for God is 'all in all',[12] and this applies to the church, where like in friendship, 'many are one'.[13] The mode of divine presence, and of longing to be, is not restricted for Augustine to the mode of the gift, for God is 'all in all'. Augustine recognized this soon after baptism, as he plunged into the depths of interiority to search for God in the mysterious and spacious chambers of memory, 'a place that is no place'.[14] He inquiries of God, 'Where did I find you, so that I could learn you?'[15] God is master even of space and time; thus limits do not restrict God, as Augustine comes to realize: 'It is nowhere, this "place"; and though we approach it and draw back from it, it is nowhere, a place that is no place.'[16] The same is the case for God's abode, 'the holy Church diffused throughout the world'.[17] Augustine follows Paul closely on this, 'For just as the body is one and has many members, and all the members of the body, though many, are one body, so it is with Christ.'[18] 'God with us' and 'God for us' do not separate the Eucharist and the priests from the church and the faithful by a mere act of physical distance, as Solari suggests. For Augustine, just as the incarnation ('God with us') goes in hand with redemption ('God for us'), and just as the historical Jesus cannot be divorced from his mission as the Christ of salvation, so too the church as the body of Christ flows flawlessly from the sacrament of the cross. Augustine writes, 'We too are fed from the Lord's Cross . . . [because] we eat his body.'[19] This means the cross is accessible in the sacraments. Augustine also notes,

> The bread which you can see on the altar, sanctified by the word of God, is the body of Christ. That cup, or rather what the cup contains, sanctified by the word of God, is the blood of Christ. [. . .] If you receive them well, you are yourselves what you receive. The Apostle therefore says: *For we, being many, are one bread, one body.* (1 Cor 10.17)[20]

The focus is not in presence but in *becoming one*, by enjoining the continuity of Jesus the Christ from the cross to the sufferings of his body, the church, today. 'God with us' is 'God for us'. Belonging, accordingly, consists in recognizing this organic, living continuity of longing to be in the church and as church, across space and time, for all times, in all places. The formula by Vincent of Lérins, later adopted by the illustrious John Henry Newman, aptly captures the continuity of the church, from the pierced side of Christ on the cross, to wherever the believer may be: 'always, everywhere, and by everyone'.[21] Accordingly, 'God with us' is 'God for us' irrespective of distance – spiritual, temporal and spatial.

Deconfining sight

Failure to recognize 'God with us' as 'God for us', and therefore any itinerary of deconfinement that bifurcates these, is due to a loss of faith in the invisible due to the pandemic. What is the road forward? Solari appeals to synodality – an ecclesial form of governance where all walk together. This view, however, need not result in the church being the bearer of God, which is what Solari offers as the promise of Easter:

> Easter approaches. God wants to be with us. As through the tomb, may his resurrection bring him through all [virtual] screens. [. . .] let us open our doors – the doors of our homes, to the One who dwells alone in the tabernacles, to the One who does not want and has never wanted to be without us. Without his community. Without his brothers and sisters. Pastors, our brothers, come forth in your turn. From your chapels, from your schemes. Bring the Eucharist to families and homes, so that the Lord is not alone. So that at Easter we can say in truth that 'when evening came on that day, the first of the week, and the doors of the place where the disciples were, were shut for fear of the virus, Jesus came and stood among them' (Jn 20.19).[22]

Solari's approach is particularly appealing for a time of confinement, where a quarantined church spontaneously longs for the solidarity of presence, for a return to normalcy, instinctively seeking venues to begin moving forward after a year of painstakingly questioning, reconsidering and adapting social life.

However, Solari's position is motivated by a suspicion of the invisible. This past year, the deadly effects of an invisible pathogen have raised awareness of the reality of invisible things: death, isolation, distancing and separation. For this reason, recognizing the power of the invisible in the context of this pandemic has come at the price of mistakenly conflating absence with invisibility. Consequently, touch as the metaphor for overcoming the absence of distance has become the spontaneous response to contest the eroding power of the invisible, such as in the case of vouching for solidarity as the antidote to longing in the midst of the invisible. This misses the mark, however. In an itinerary of deconfinement, the necessary recovery of the invisible is irreducible to suspicion and irrespective of presence or absence. An itinerary of deconfinement, of learning to dwell anew in longing to be a church, consists in recovering the invisible by learning to trust the invisible and therefore to appreciate the presence of distance in the making of church. The invisibility of distance reveals following Augustine that in longing to be or in be-longing, sight primes over touch because the church arises as the manifestation of belonging from the passage of invisibility to the horizon of endless possibilities, precisely because what God sees, everything, *is*. All things are, as Augustine writes, because God sees them: 'so we see the things you have made because they are, but they are because you see them.'[23] Augustine eloquently longs for sight in writing: 'Do not hide your face from me. Let me die, lest I die, that I might see your face.'[24]

Being the times

The church is present in the midst of and despite social distancing, for the community of worship is not what constitutes the unity of the church but is, on the contrary, a sign of a deeper communion, which precedes and supersedes spatiotemporal presence. Augustine's words after the sacking of Rome in 410 suitably capture the essentials of belonging during the time of the pandemic: 'the times are troubled, that's what people say. Let us live good lives, and the times are good. We ourselves are the times. Whatever we are like, that's what the times are like.'[25] The sacrament of belonging in the church pours forth into the horizon of visibility from within the mysterious depth of the cross, through the pierced side of the crucified. The church is manifested *where* the believer is, *as* the believer is. It is united by grace and flows from the mystery of the body of Christ, the church. Added to the various challenges the church faces today, the pandemic is an invitation to appreciate anew the centrality of the believer as an icon of God's divine presence and as the boundless epicentre of belonging in the community of the church. In a world of despair, the voice of Christ echoes the cry of a church in distress, awaiting deliverance, yet consoled by the reminder that God is there, that God has always been there, in the midst of it all, where deliverance has already been accomplished. Augustine conveys this confidence: 'It is necessary for his body, the church, to endure temptations in this world, but its consoler is never absent. He has promised, *Lo, I am with you throughout all days, even to the end of the ages* (Mt 28:20).'[26]

NOTES

Introduction

1 The book is an adaptation and extension, in form and content, of Pablo Irizar, 'Where Is the Church? Augustine on Belonging as Unbound Images of God in the Church', *Louvain Studies* 44 (4): 2020. Large portions of the original text have been reproduced with the permission of the author and publisher.

2 Friedrich Nietzsche, *The Gay Science*, trans. Walter Kaufmann (New York: Vintage, 1974), 181–2.

3 Gregory Solari, '*Ecclesia*: Absence réelle', *La Croix*, 6 April 2020, URL: https://faire-eglise.blogs.la-croix.com/absence-reelle/2020/04/06/: 'Nous nous voulons « solidaires ». Solidaires avec les malades, avec les familles affectées, avec le monde en souffrance. Solidaires, y compris quand tout contact social est empêché, comme aujourd'hui – solidaires, envers et contre tout, à distance. Solidaires, quand bien même la solidarité est impossible, sinon comme un discours.'

4 Ibid: 'La solidarité se nourrit de communion « de désir », qu'alimentent à distance les messes mises en ligne sur les sites de nos Églises. Solidaires, doublement, avec ceux qui ne peuvent pas communier habituellement, et solidaires avec les prêtres qui, eux, peuvent communier quotidiennement, dans des célébrations sans communauté, sinon virtuelle.'

5 Ibid: 'Dès lors, pourquoi, dans ces conditions, plutôt que de tenir à distance les baptisés, et ainsi d'entretenir une représentation obsolète de l'Eglise, avec sa bipartition – pourquoi ne pas profiter de ce confinement pour confier l'Eucharistie aux fidèles baptisés, aux familles qui le désirent ? Pourquoi ne pas profiter de ce confinement pour responsabiliser les baptisés plutôt que de les maintenir dans cette posture passive vis-à-vis des pasteurs et d'une pastorale pensée par et finalement pour les pasteurs ? Un peu de cohérence : on ne peut pas d'un côté chanter les louanges du Peuple de Dieu, renchérir sur la dignité des baptisés, défendre à grands cris la beauté de la famille, chrétienne ou non, et en même temps refuser que les foyers

chrétiens puissent devenir de petites églises domestiques – des *Ecclesiola*. Imagine-t-on le « poids de grâce » que cela constituerait pour les multiples familles, qui accueillant l'Eucharistie y trouveraient leur force dans la violence de l'épreuve et deviendraient autant de reposoirs au cœur du monde, des quartiers, des campagnes, et non plus dans la solitude d'une église verrouillée ?'

6 *conf.* 10.8, CCL 27, 159. Williams, 67.
7 *conf.* 8.29, CCL 27, 131. Williams, 137.
8 Possidius, *Life of Augustine*, H. T. Weiskotten, *Sancti Augustini Vita scripta a Possidio Episcopo*, 1919, http://www.tertullian.org/fathers/possidius_life_of_augustine_02_text.htm#C31 (accessed 18 March 2021).
9 Matt 26.41.
10 *conf.* 8.17, CCL 27, 124. Williams, 131.
11 *conf.* 10.40, CCL 27, 176. Williams, 184.
12 *conf.* 1.7, CCL 27, 3–4. Williams, 4.
13 *conf.* 10.50, CCL 27, 181–2. Williams, 190.
14 *conf.* 10.7, CCL 27, 158. Williams, 166.
15 *conf.* 3.11, CCL 27, 32–3. Williams, 35.
16 *conf.* 10.7, CCL 27, 158. Williams, 166.
17 *conf.* 3.1, CCL 27, 27. Williams, 29.
18 *conf.* 1.1, CCL 27, 1. Williams, 1.
19 Ex 3.14.
20 *conf.* 7.13, CCL 27, 101.
21 *conf.* 10.1, CCL 27, 155.
22 *conf.* 3.17, CCL 27, 40.
23 *s.* 165.3, PL 38, 903–4. WSA III/5, 202–3.
24 *conf.* 13.53, CCL 27, 272. Williams, 277–8.
25 Jn 20.27.
26 Lk. 18.41.

Chapter 1

1 Lk. 24.39.
2 William E. Connolly, *Identity, Difference: Democratic Negotiations of Political Paradox* (Minnesota: University of Minnesota Press,

2002), 167; Kathleen R. Skerrett, '*Consuetudo carnalis* in Augustine's *Confessions*: Confessing Identity/Belonging to Difference', *Journal of Religious Ethics* 37, no. 3 (2009): 496.

3 Vincent Giraud, '*Signum* et *vestigium* dans la pensée de saint Augustin', *Revue des sciences philosophiques et théologiques* 5, no. 2 (2011): 251–74, esp. 254.

4 Carl W. Griffin and David L. Paulsen, 'Augustine and the Corporeality of God', *Harvard Theological Review* 95, no. 1 (2002): 114.

5 Jean Damascène, *Discours contre ceux qui disent du mal des images* (*Contra imaginum calumniatores*), I, 16, PG XCIV, col. 1245. Emmanuel Falque, *The Phenomenology of Christ in Flesh and Bones*, https://churchlifejournal.nd.edu/articles/christ-in-the-flesh-and-bone/ (accessed 21 March 2021).

6 *conf.* 7.13, CCL 27, 101. Williams, 108.

7 *sol.* 2.13, CSEL 89, 61–3. Cleveland, 48.

8 *sol.* 2.13, CSEL 89, 61–3. Cleveland, 50.

9 Gen. 1.26. *The English Standard Version Bible* (New York, 2009).

10 *Acad.* 3.37, CCL 29, 57.

11 *sol.* 1.4, CSEL 89, 7–9.

12 *conf.* 7.16, CCL 27, 103.

13 Ibid.

14 *nat. b.* 27, CSEL 25, 868.

15 Matthew Drever, 'Redeeming Creation: *Creatio ex nihilo* and the *imago dei* in Augustine', *International Journal of Systematic Theology* 15, no. 2 (2013): 120.

16 Ibid.

17 *conf.* 1.7, CCL 27, 3–4. Williams, 4.

18 *ciu.* 11.26, CCL 48, 345–6. Dyson, 484.

19 *conf.* 7.24, CCL 27, 108.

20 *conf.* 7.23, CCL 27, 107.

21 Col. 1.15.

22 Ibid.

23 *diu. qu.* 74, CCL 44/A, 213–4. WSA I/12, 137. Robert A. Markus, '*imago* and *similitudo* in Augustine', *Revue d'Etudes Augustiniennes et Patristiques* 10, nos 2–3 (1964): 125–43.

24 *conf.* 3.12, CCL 27, 33. Williams, 36.

25 *conf.* 5.24, CCL 27, 71. Williams, 77.
26 *conf.* 6.6, CCL 27, 77. Williams, 81–2.
27 *Ex.* 6.45, PL 14:259-60. Ambrose, *Hexameron, Paradise, Cain and Abel, The Fathers of the Church*, trans. John J. Savage (Washington: The Catholic University of America Press, 1961), 257.
28 *Ex.* 6.45, PL 14:259-60. *Hexameron*, 256.
29 *conf.* 6.4, CCL 27, 76. *Confessions*, 81–2.
30 *Gn. litt. inp.* 16.62, CSEL 26, 502–3.
31 *Gn. litt.* 3.34, CSEL 28, 88–90.
32 *trin.* 12.12, CCL 50, 366–7.
33 *trin.* 12.10, CCL 50, 364–5.
34 *conf.* 13.47, CCL 27, 270.
35 *adult. coniug.* 2.21, CSEL 41, 408–9.
36 *Io. eu. tr.* 121.1, CCL 36, 664–5. George Lawless, '*infirmior sexus . . . fortiori affectus*: Augustine's *Jo. ev. tr.* 121.1-3: Mary Magdalene', *Augustinian Studies* 34 (2003): 107–18.
37 *conf.* 1.1, CCL 27, 1.
38 Ex. 3.14.
39 *ciu.* 11.9, CCL 48, 337–8.
40 *conf.* 5.20, CCL 27, 68–9.
41 *conf.* 7.24, CCL 27, 108.
42 *conf.* 10.25, CCL 27, 167–8.
43 Ibid.
44 *conf.* 1.1, CCL 27, 1.
45 *conf.* 3.11, CCL 27, 32–3. Williams, 35.
46 *conf.* 10.1, CCL 27, 155. Williams, 163.
47 *conf.* 10.41, CCL 27, 176–7. Williams, 185.
48 *conf.* 10.15, CCL 27, 162–3. Williams, 170–1.
49 *conf.* 3.11, CCL 27, 32–3. Williams, 35.
50 *conf.* 1.7, CCL 27, 3–4. Williams, 4.
51 Roland J. Teske, *Paradoxes of Time in Saint Augustine* (Marquette: Marquette University Press, 1996), 22.
52 *conf.* 11.17, CCL 27, 203.
53 *cons. phil.* 5.6. Boethius, *Consolation of Philosophy*, trans. Joel C. Relihan (Indianapolis: Hackett Publishing, 2001), 144.
54 *conf.* 1.7, CCL 27, 3–4. Williams, 4.

Chapter 2

1 *Gn. litt. inp.* 16.61. CSEL 28, 501–3. WSA I/13, 150–1.
2 Ibid.
3 *conf.* 13.32, CCL 27, 260–1. Williams, 267.
4 Ibid.
5 *trin.* 9.18, CCL 50, 309–10. Augustine, *On the Trinity*, ed. Gareth Matthews and trans. Stephen McKenna (Cambridge: Cambridge University Press, 2002), 40. Also, *trin.* 12.4, CCL 50, 358.
6 *trin.* 9.18, CCL 50, 309–10. Matthews and McKenna, 40. Also, *trin.* 12.4, CCL 50, 358.
7 *trin.* 15.21, CCL 50A, 490.
8 *ciu.* 11.26, CCL 48, 45–6. Dyson, 483–4.
9 *sol.* 2.8, CSEL 89, 55–7.
10 *conf.* 11.17, CCL 27, 203.
11 *ciu.* 11.26, CCL 48, 45–6. Dyson, 484.
12 Maarten Wisse, *Trinitarian Theology beyond Participation: Augustine's De Trinitate and Contemporary Theology* (London: T&T Clark, 2011), 148–9.
13 Roland Kany, *Augustins Trinitätsdenken* (Tübingen: Mohr Siebeck, 2007), 508. Wisse, *Trinitarian Theology beyond Participation*, 154.
14 *ciu.* 11.26, CCL 48, 45–6. Dyson, 484.
15 *trin.* 14.15, CCL 50A, 442.
16 *conf.* 4. 28, CCL 27, 54. WSA I/1, 109–10.
17 Ibid.
18 Aristotle, *Categories*, 1b25. Paul Studtmann, 'Aristotle's Categories', in *The Stanford Encyclopedia of Philosophy* (Spring 2021 Edition), ed. Edward N. Zalta, forthcoming URL https://plato.stanford.edu/archives/spr2021/entries/aristotle-categories/.
19 Aristotle, *Categories*, 1b25–2a4.
20 *conf.* 4. 28, CCL 27, 54. WSA I/1, 109–10.
21 *conf.* 4. 29, CCL 27, 54–5. WSA I/1, 109–10.
22 Jean-Luc Marion, 'Notes sur l'usage de *substantia* par saint Augustin et sur son appartenance à l'histoire de la métaphysique', in *Mots médiévaux offerts à Ruedi Imbach*, eds. I. Atucha, D. Calma, C. König-Pralong and I. Zavatter (Porto: Fédération internationale des Instituts d'études médiévales, 2011), 501.

23 Aristotle, *Categories* 7, 6a36–6b.
24 Aristotle, *Categories* 7, 8a29–35.
25 Aristotle, *Categories* 7, 8a28–33. Matthew Duncombe, *Ancient Relativity: Plato, Aristotle, Stoics, and Sceptics* (Oxford: Oxford University Press, 2020), 125.
26 *trin.* 5.6, CCL 50, 210. WSA I/5, 233.
27 Ibid.
28 Ibid.
29 1 Jn 4.8.
30 *trin.* 7.4, CCL 50, 251. WSA I/5, 275.
31 *conf.* 11.17, CCL 27, 203.
32 *trin.* 3.4, CCL 50, 130. WSA I/5, 276–7.
33 The Latin word *infans* means speechless.
34 *conf.* 1.13, CCL 27, 7. Williams, 8.
35 Ibid.
36 *Gn. adu. Man.* 2.9, CSEL 91, 128. WSA I/13, 77.
37 Ibid.
38 Ibid.
39 Ibid.
40 *Gn. litt. inp.* 16.60, CSEL 28, 500–1. WSA I/13, 149–50.
41 *Gn. adu. Man.* 1.28, CSEL 91, 95–6. WSA I/13, 68.
42 *doctr. chr.* 2.1, Augustinus, *De doctrina Christiana*, ed. M. Simonetti (Verona, 1994), 74. Stephan Meier-Oeser, 'Medieval Semiotics', in *The Stanford Encyclopedia of Philosophy* (Summer 2011 Edition), ed. Edward N. Zalta, URL https://plato.stanford.edu/archives/sum2011/entries/semiotics-medieval/.
43 *trin.* 14.24, CCL 50, 456. CTHP, 164.
44 Ibid.
45 *trin.* 14.24, CCL 50, 455–6. CTHP, 163–4.
46 Ibid.
47 *en. Ps.* 66.4, CCL 39, 861. WSA III/17, 313–14.
48 Ibid.
49 *en. Ps.* 138.2, CCL 40, 1990–1. WSA III/20, 257.

Chapter 3

1 *conf.* 10.1, CCL 27, 155.
2 *sol.* 2.1, CSEL 89, 45.

3 Ibid.
4 *conf.* 3.2, CCL 27, 27. Williams, 30.
5 Ibid.
6 Ibid.
7 Ibid.
8 *conf.* 3.3, CCL 27, 27. Williams, 30.
9 *conf.* 3.21, CCL 27, 38–9. Williams, 42.
10 *conf.* 9.14, CCL 27, 140–1. Williams, 147–8.
11 Ibid.
12 *conf.* 10.49, CCL 27, 181.
13 *conf.* 10.49, CCL 27, 181. Williams, 190.
14 *conf.* 10.50, CCL 27, 181–2. Williams, 189–90.
15 Rowan Williams, 'Augustine and the Psalms', *Interpretation* 58, no. 1 (2004): 17–27.
16 Ibid., 18.
17 *en. Ps.* 85.1, CCL 39, 1176. WSA III/18, 220-1.
18 Michael Fiedrowicz, *Psalmus vox totius Christi. Studien zu Augustins Enarrationes in Psalmos* (Freiburg: Herder, 1997).
19 Maria Boulding, 'St Augustine's View of the Psalms as a Communion of Faith between Generations', *The Downside Review* 126 (2008): 128.
20 Athanasius, *De incarnatione verbi dei* 54.3, PG 25, 192B.
21 *en. Ps.* 42.1, PL 36, 476. WSA III/16, 266.
22 *en. Ps.* 85.1, CCL 39, 1176. WSA III/18, 220–1.
23 Boulding, 'St Augustine's View of the Psalms as a Communion of Faith between Generations', 126.
24 *en. Ps.* 86.5, CCL 39, 1202. WSA III/18, 251.
25 *en. Ps.* 86.5, CCL 39, 1202. WSA III/18, 250–1.
26 Ibid.
27 *en. Ps.* 94.1, PL 37, 1472. WSA III/18, 409.
28 Lk. 23.34.
29 *en. Ps.* 93.8, CCL 39, 1311. WSA III/18, 384.
30 *en. Ps.* 93.8, CCL 39, 1311. WSA III/18, 385.
31 Ibid.
32 *en. Ps.* 93.8, CCL 39, 1311. WSA III/18, 383.
33 *en. Ps.* 93.8, CCL 39, 1311. WSA III/18, 383–4.

34 Lk. 23.43.
35 *en. Ps.* 39.15, CCL 38, 437, WSA III/16, 210–1.
36 Ibid.
37 Ibid.
38 Ibid.
39 Jn 19.26-27.
40 *Io eu. tr.* 119.1, CCL 36, 658. WSA III/13, 499.
41 Ibid.
42 Matt. 27.46 and Mk 15.34.
43 *en. Ps.* 37.6, CCL 38, 386. WSA III/16, 150.
44 Ibid.
45 Ibid.
46 Ibid.
47 *en. Ps.* 37.6, CCL 38, 386. WSA III/16, 150–1.
48 Jn 19.28.
49 *Io eu. tr.* 17.15, 178. WSA III/12, 317.
50 Ibid.
51 *Io eu. tr.* 17.15, 178. WSA III/12, 318.
52 *Io eu. tr.* 37.9, CCL 36, 337. WSA III/12, 573.
53 Ibid.
54 *Io eu. tr.* 17.15, 178. WSA III/12, 318.
55 *Io eu. tr.* 17.15, CCL 36, 178. WSA III/12, 573.
56 *Io eu. tr.* 17.15, CCL 36, 178. WSA III/12, 574.
57 Jn 19.30.
58 *en. ps.* 86.5, CCL 39, 1202. WSA III/18, 250.
59 *en. Ps.* 86.5, CCL 39, 1202. WSA III/18, 250–1.
60 *en. Ps.* 86.5, CCL 39, 1202. WSA III/18, 251.
61 Lk. 23.46.
62 *s.* 319.5, PL 38, 1441. WSA III/19, 153.
63 *trin.* 4.5, CCL 50, 165. WSA I/5, 185–6.

Chapter 4

1 *s.* 165.3, PL 38, 903–4. WSA III/5, 202–3.
2 This section draws, in form and content, from the discussion of Eph 3.18 in Pablo Irizar, 'Scriptural Exegesis or Speculative

Philosophy: Augustine on the Figure of the Cross as a Paradigm of Manifestation,' NZSTh 2021; 63(3): 1–24. Some of the material has been reproduced with the permission of the publisher.

3 Ibid.
4 Geoffery D. Dunn, *Tertullian* (New York: Routledge, 2004), 37; Griffin and Paulsen, 'Augustine and the Corporeality of God', 97–118; George Christopher Stead, 'Divine Substance in Tertullian', *The Journal of Theological Studies* 14 (1963): 46–66; Petr Kitzler, 'Tertullian's Concept of the Soul and His Corporealistic Ontology', *Wiener Studien* 122 (2009): 145–69.
5 *sol.* 2.33, CSEL 89, 92–3. Burleigh, 60.
6 Ibid.
7 Ibid.
8 *mus.* 6.17, Jacobsson, 40.
9 Ibid.
10 *mus.* 6.18, Jacobsson, 41–2.
11 Joeph Torchia, Creatio ex nihilo *and the Theology of St. Augustine: The Anti-Manichaean Polemic and Beyond* (New York: Peter Lang, 1999).
12 *mus.* 6.17, Jacobsson, 40.
13 *s.* 165.3, PL 38, 903–4. WSA III/5, 202–3.
14 *diu. qu.* 57.2, CCL 44A, 98–101. WSA I/12, 73.
15 *an. quant.* 4.6, CSEL 89, 137–9. FC, 65.
16 Ibid.
17 Ibid.
18 Ibid.
19 *an. quant.* 5.7, CSEL 89, 139–40. FC, 66.
20 *an. quant.* 5.8, CSEL 89, 139–40. FC, 68.
21 *an. quant.* 5.9, CSEL 89, 139–40. FC, 69.
22 *an. quant.* 13, CSEL 89, 145–7. FC, 83.
23 *trin.* 10.10, CCL 50, 323–4. WSA I/5, 372.
24 *diu. qu.* 20, CCL 44A, 25. WSA I/12, 38.
25 Ibid.
26 1 Cor. 15.28.
27 *s.* 165.3, PL 38, 903–4. WSA III/5, 202–3.
28 Col. 1.15.

29 Markus Barth, *Ephesians/1 Introduction, Translation, and Commentary on Chapters 1-3* (Doubleday, 1974), 395–6.
30 *an. quant.* 4.6, CSEL 89, 137–9. FC, 65.
31 Ibid.
32 Ibid.
33 Ibid.
34 *an. quant.* 5.7, CSEL 89, 139–40. FC, 66.
35 Ibid.
36 Ibid.
37 Ibid.
38 *an. quant.* 5.8, CSEL 89, 139–40. FC, 68.
39 *an. quant.* 5.9, CSEL 89, 139–40. FC, 69.
40 *an. quant.* 11, CSEL 89, 143–4. FC, 80.
41 *an. quant.* 11, CSEL 89, 144–5. FC, 81.
42 *an. quant.* 13, CSEL 89, 145–7. FC, 83.
43 *trin.* 10.9, CCL 50, 322–3. WSA I/5, 371.
44 Ibid.
45 Ibid. See footnote, 14 in WSA I/5, 371: citing *De Caelo* 1.2, 269 at *Tusc. Disp.* 1.12, 26, Cicero mistakenly ascribes the fifth material element to Aristotle.
46 *trin.* 10.9, CCL 50, 322–3. WSA I/5, 372.
47 Ibid.
48 *trin.* 10.10, CCL 50, 323–4. WSA I/5, 372.
49 *Gn. litt. inp.* 16.60, CSEL 28, 500–1. WSA I/13, 149–50.
50 *diu. qu.* 20, CCL 44A, 25. WSA I/12, 38.
51 Ibid.
52 *conf.* 13.53, CCL 27, 272. Williams, 277–8.
53 *diu. qu.* 57.2, CCL 44A, 98–101. WSA I/12, 73.
54 Ibid.
55 *ciu.* 15.27, CCL 48, 495–7. WSA I/7, 183.
56 *mor.* 1.33, CSEL 90, 37–8.
57 Augustine foils the Passover at Ex. 12.22 with 1 Cor. 5.7, as a foretelling of the sacrifice of Christ.
58 *doctr. chr.* 2.62, 165–6. WSA I/11, 172.

59 Ibid.
60 *en. Ps.* 51.12 and *s.* 72.
61 *diu. qu.* 68.2, CCL 44A, 175–7. WSA I/12, 116.
62 *ep.* 55.25, CSEL 34, 196–8. WSA II/1, 228–9.
63 *ep.* 140.64, CSEL 44, 211–12. WSA II/2, 277.
64 Ibid. Robert Dodaro, *Christ and the Just Society in the Thought of Augustine* (Cambridge: Cambridge University Press, 2004), 164.
65 *ep.* 147.18, CSEL 44, 289–92. WSA II/2, 327–8.
66 Jn 14.9.
67 Eph. 3.18.
68 *ep.* 140.64, CSEL 44, 211–12. WSA II/2, 277.
69 *ep.* 140.63, CSEL 44, 209–11. WSA II/2, 275–6.
70 Ibid.
71 Ibid.
72 Ibid.
73 Matt. 16.16-19.
74 For a sustained discussion of these passages, see Pablo Irizar, 'A Quarantined Church? Augustine on Belonging in the Church as Unbound Images of God', *Louvain Studies* 44, no. 4 (2020): 315–34; 'Augustine on the Metamorphosis of Interiority', in Alexandra Grund-Wittenberg (ed.), *Religious Practice and Individuality* (forthcoming, 2021); 'Sensing Dislocated Belonging. Augustine on the Church as the Image of God in the *Expositions on the Psalms*', *Studies in Spirituality* (forthcoming, 2021); 'Many as One. Augustine's Onefold Ecclesiology', *International Journal of Philosophy and Theology* (forthcoming 2021).
75 Daniel Cardó, *The Cross and the Eucharist in Early Christianity: A Theological and Liturgical Investigation* (Cambridge: Cambridge University Press, 2019), 29.
76 *en. Ps.* 100.9, CCL 39, 1414. WSA III/19, 39.
77 *s.* 227.1, SC 116, 234–42. WSA III/6, 254. Cardó, *The Cross*, 37.
78 *s. Denis* 3.3 = *s.* 228B.3, MA 2, 19–20. WSA III/6, 261–2. Cardó, *The Cross*, 17.
79 *s. Denis* 3.2 = *s.* 228B.2, MA 2, 19, 19–20. WSA III/6, 261–2.
80 *s.* 165.3, PL 38, 903–4. WSA III/5, 202–3.
81 Ibid.

Chapter 5

1. Virgil, *Georgics* 3.284.
2. Marcel Proust, *In Search of Lost Time: The Way by Swann's* (Penguin UK, 2003).
3. Emmanuel Falque, *The Metamorphosis of Finitude: An Essay on Birth and Resurrection* (New York: Fordham University Press, 2012), 78.
4. *conf.* 13.53, CCL 27, 272. Williams, 277–8.
5. *conf.* 11.39, CCL 27, 214–5. Williams, 222.
6. Jn 1.14.
7. Falque, *The Metamorphosis of Finitude*, 20.
8. Ibid., 112.
9. Richard Kearney and Brian Treanor, eds. *Carnal Hermeneutics* (New York: Fordham University Press, 2015), 1.
10. Ibid., 112.
11. Ibid., 24.
12. *Ethics*, Part V, *Prop.* XXIII, *Scholium.* See, Spinoza, *Ethics*, trans. Edwin Curley, *The Collected Writings of Spinoza* (Princeton: Princeton University Press, 1985), vol. 1.
13. Falque, *The Metamorphosis of Finitude*, 22.
14. Jean Guitton, *Le temps et l'éternité chez Plotin et Saint Augustin* (Paris: Vrin, 2004).
15. Falque, *The Metamorphosis of Finitude*, 22.
16. Susannah Ticciati, *A New Apophaticism: Augustine and the Redemption of Signs* (Leiden: Brill, 2013).
17. David Van Dusen, *The Space of Time: A Sensualist Interpretation of Time in Augustine: Confessions X to XII* (Leiden: Brill, 2014).
18. Marion, 'Notes sur l'usage de *substantia* par saint Augustin et sur son appartenance à l'histoire de la métaphysique', 507.
19. Kari Kloos, *Christ, Creation, and the Vision of God: Augustine's Transformation of Early Christian Theophany Interpretation* (Leiden: Brill, 2010).
20. John C. Cavadini, '*Time* and *Ascent* in *Confessions XI*," in *Collectanea Augustiniana 2: Presbyter Factus Sum*, edited by J. Lienhard, E. Muller and R. Teske (Peter Lang, 1993), 171–85. Frederick E. Van Fleteren, 'Augustine's Ascent of the Soul in Book VII of the Confessions: A Reconsideration', *Augustinian Studies* 5 (1974): 29–72.

21 Katherin A. Rogers, 'St. Augustine on Time and Eternity', *American Catholic Philosophical Quarterly* 70, no. 2 (1996): 207–23.
22 Torrance W. J. Kirby, 'Praise as the Soul's Overcoming of Time in the *Confessions* of St. Augustine', *Pro Ecclesia* 6, no. 3 (1997): 333–50.
23 Simo Knuuttila, 'Time and Creation in Augustine', *The Cambridge Companion to Augustine*, ed. Vincent Meconi and Eleonore Stump (Cambridge: Cambridge University Press, 2001), 103–15, esp. 109–13.
24 Robert Jordan, 'Time and contingency in St. Augustine', *The Review of Metaphysics* 8, no. 3 (1955): 394–417, esp. 394; James Wetzel, 'Time after Augustine', *Religious Studies* 31, no. 1 (1995): 341–57.
25 Marilyn Ekdahl Ravicz, 'St Augustine: Time and Eternity', *The Thomist* 22, no. 4 (1959): 542–54.
26 John L. Morrison, 'Augustine's Two Theories of Time', *The New Scholasticism* 45, no. 4 (1971): 600–10; Wilma G. Von Jess, 'Augustine', *The New Scholasticism* 46, no. 3 (1972): 337–51.
27 *Enneads* 3.8.4. Plato, *Symposium* 203b-c.
28 1 Jn 2.16. Williams, xxvii.
29 *conf.* 1.7, CCL 27, 3–4. Williams, 4.
30 1 Cor. 13.1-8.
31 *conf.* 10.38, CCL 27, 175. Williams, 183.
32 Teske, *Paradoxes of Time in Saint Augustine*.
33 *conf.* 11.13, CCL 27, 200–1.
34 Ibid., 10. *conf.* 11.12, CCL 27, 200.
35 Teske, *Paradoxes of Time in Saint Augustine*, 17.
36 *ep.* 18, CSEL 34, 44–5.
37 Teske, *Paradoxes of Time in Saint Augustine*, 22.
38 *conf.* 12.7, CCL 27, 219.
39 *cons. phil.* 5.6. Boethius, *Consolation of Philosophy*, 144.
40 *en. Ps.* 134.6.
41 *conf.* 11.6, CCL 27, 197. Williams, 205.
42 *conf.* 1.3, CCL 27, 2–3.
43 Emmanuel Falque, *God, the Flesh and the Other: From Iraneus to Duns Scotus* (Evanston: Northwestern University Press, 2014), 25.
44 Marion, 'Notes sur l'usage de *substantia* par saint Augustin et sur son appartenance à l'histoire de la métaphysique', 507.

45 *conf.* 11.17, CCL 27, 202. Williams, 210.
46 Teske, *Paradoxes of Time in Saint Augustine*, 23.
47 Ibid., 24. *conf.* 11.17, CCL 27, 203.
48 Plato, *Timaeus*, 38°.
49 *conf.* 11.23, CCL 27, 205–6. Williams, 213.
50 *conf.* 11.26, CCL 27, 206–7. Williams, 214.
51 *conf.* 9.20, CCL 27, 145–6. Williams, 153.
52 *conf.* 11.36, CCL 27, 213. Williams, 220–1.
53 *conf.* 11.30, CCL 27, 209. Williams, 217.
54 *conf.* 11.39, CCL 27, 214. Williams, 222.
55 *en. Ps.* 148.8.
56 *en. Ps.* 101.14.
57 *conf.* 11.9, CCL 27, 198–9.
58 *mus.* 6.29, Jacobsson, Martin and Lukas Dorfbauer, 'Augustinus, De Musica (CSEL 102)'. (2017), 66.
59 *ord.* 2.14, CSEL 63, 156. Nancy van Deusen, 'De Musica', in Allan Fitzgerald and Jaroslav Jan Pelikan, *Augustine through the Ages: An Encyclopedia* (Grand Rapids: Eerdmans Publishing, 1999), 572.
60 Elena Lombardi, *The Syntax of Desire: Language and Love in Augustine, the Modistae, Dante* (Toronto: University of Toronto Press, 2007), 48.
61 *conf.* 11.7, CCL 27, 197–9.
62 *ord.* 2.14, CSEL 63, 156.
63 *mus.* 3.4, PL 32, 1117.
64 *conf.* 11.26, CCL 27, 206–7. Williams, 214–15.
65 *mus.* 5.3, PL 32, 1148–9.
66 *mus.* 5.4, PL 32, 1149.
67 *ord.* 2.14, CSEL 63, 156.
68 J. L. Austin, *How to Do Things with Words*, ed. J. O. Urmson and Marina Sbisá (Cambridge, MA: Harvard University Press, 1962).
69 Ibid., 5–6.
70 *conf.* 10.1, CCL 27, 155.
71 *ord.* 1.3, CSEL 63, 122–3.
72 *ord.* 2.18, CSEL 63, 158–9.
73 Gen. 1.1.

74 *conf.* 12.40, CCL 27, 238–40. Williams, 245.
75 Frederick Van Fleteren, 'Matter' in Allan Fitzgerald, *Augustine through the Ages: An Encyclopedia* (Grand Rapids: Eerdmans Publishing, 1999), 547–9.
76 *ord.* 2.16, *nat. b.* 27. Also, Van Fleteren, 'Matter', 547.
77 *conf.* 12.14, CCL 27, 222–3.
78 *Gn. litt.* 1.15.
79 *conf.* 12.6, CCL 27, 218–19.
80 Van Fleteren, 'Matter', 148.
81 *conf.* 12.3, CCL 27, 217–8. Williams, 203.
82 *conf.* 12.6, CCL 27, 218–9. Williams, 226.
83 *conf.* 12.18, CCL 27, 224–5. Williams, 232.
84 *conf.* 12.15, CCL 27, 223. Williams, 230.
85 *conf.* 12. 15, CCL 27, 223. Williams, 231.
86 *conf.* 12.14, CCL 27, 222–3. Williams, 230.
87 *conf.* 12.15, CCL 27, 223. Williams, 231.
88 *conf.* 12.40, CCL 27, 238–40. Williams, 245.
89 Ibid.
90 Ibid.
91 *conf.* 12.40, CCL 27, 238–40. Williams, 245–6.
92 *conf.* 12.40, CCL 27, 238–40. Williams, 246.
93 Ibid., 246.
94 Carl Johann Perl and Alan Kriegsman, 'Augustine and Music: On the Occasion of the 1600th Anniversary of the Saint', *The Musical Quarterly* 41, no. 4 (October 1955): 189.
95 Plato, *Timaeus* 37c-e.
96 Eph. 5.16.
97 *conf.* 12.1, CCL 27, 217.
98 Wis. 7.27.
99 *conf.* 7.17, CCL 27, 104. Williams, 110.
100 Falque, *The Metamorphosis of Finitude*, 114.
101 Ibid., 117.
102 Rom. 8.24.
103 *s.* 80.8, PL 38, 498. WSA III/3, 355–6.
104 Proust, *In Search of Lost Time*, Vol. 5/6, 171.

Conclusion

1 Georg W. F. Hegel, *Elements of the Philosophy of Right*, ed. Allen W. Wood, trans. H. B. Nisbet (Cambridge: Cambridge University Press, 1991), 23.
2 *conf.* 13.10, CCL 27, 246–7. Williams, 225.
3 *conf.* 11.39, CCL 27, 175–6. Williams, 221–2.
4 Matt. 26.41.
5 *conf.* 1.7, CCL 27, 3–4. Williams, 4.
6 *conf.* 10.50, CCL 27, 181–2. Williams, 190.
7 *s.* 165.3, PL 38, 903–4. WSA III/5, 202–3.
8 *en. Ps.* 78.4, WSA III/18, 130.
9 Solari, '*Ecclesia*: Absence réelle': 'Dieu avec qui ? On ne peut pas sans incohérence confesser que le Dieu chrétien a pour Nom « Dieu avec nous » (« Emmanuel ») et refuser que ce Dieu « pour nous », depuis toujours et pour toujours, demeure concrètement avec son peuple – avec *tout* son peuple. Une notion saine des sacrements non seulement n'interdit pas, mais implique la possibilité de recueillir cette « manne » du Seigneur dans les maisonnées chrétiennes. Dans des conditions à définir, certes, mais nous parlons du principe ici. Et puis enfin, un peu de réalisme. Que reste-t-il de l'institution ? Que va-t-il rester de nos plans pastoraux, de nos maillages territoriaux hérités d'une configuration ecclésiale et sociale aujourd'hui disparue ? Ici, il conviendrait de croiser l'insistance de Benoît XVI sur la communauté monastique comme paradigme de l'Église avec celle de François sur la synodalité comme paradigme de l'Église – de sa vie et de son agir.'
10 Is. 7.14; Matt. 1.22; Rev. 21.3.
11 Ps. 56.9.
12 1 Cor. 15.28.
13 *conf.* 4.13, CCL 27, 47.
14 *conf.* 10.37, CCL 27, 174–5. Williams, 183.
15 Ibid.
16 Ibid.
17 *en. Ps.* 37.6, CCL 38, 386. WSA III/16, 150.
18 1 Cor. 12.12.
19 *en. Ps.* 100.9, CCL 39, 1414. WSA III/19, 39.
20 *s.* 227.1, SC 116, 234–42. WSA III/6, 254. Cardó, *The Cross*, 37.

21 Thomas G. Guarino, *Vincent of Lérins and the Development of Christian Doctrine* (Grand Rapids: Baker Books, 2013), 5.
22 Solari, '*Ecclesia*: Absence réelle': 'Pâques approche. Dieu veut être avec nous. Comme à travers le tombeau, que sa resurrection le fasse traverser tous les écrans. Là où le confinement n'est pas total, en Suisse romande par exemple, ouvrons nos portes – les portes de nos maisons, à Celui qui demeure seul dans les tabernacles, à Celui qui ne se veut pas et ne s'est jamais voulu sans nous. Sans sa communauté. Sans ses frères et sœurs. Pasteurs, nos frères, sortez à votre tour. De vos chapelles, de vos schémas. Apportez l'Eucharistie dans les familles et foyers, pour que le Seigneur ne soit pas seul. Pour qu'à Pâques nous puissions dire en vérité que « *le soir étant venu ce jour-là, le premier de la semaine, les portes du lieu où étaient les disciples étant fermées par crainte du virus, Jésus vint, et se tint au milieu d'eux* » (Jn 20, 19).'
23 *conf.* 13.53, CCL 27, 272. Williams, 277–8.
24 *conf.* 1.5, CCL 27, 3. Williams, 4.
25 *s.* 80.8, PL 38, 498. WSA III/3, 355–6.
26 *en. Ps.* 94.14, CCL 39, 1341. WSA III/18, 421.

REFERENCES

Ayres, Lewis. *Augustine and the Trinity*. Cambridge: Cambridge University Press, 2010.

Berrouard, Marie-François. '*Similitudo* et la définition du réalisme sacramental d'après l'Epître XCVIII, 9-10 de saint Augustin', *Revue d'Études Augustiniennes et Patristiques* 7, no. 4 (1961): 321–37.

Bochet, Isabelle. 'Imago', in *Augustinus-Lexikon*, Vol. 3, cols. 507–19, Fasc. 1 / 2, Figura(e) – Hieronymus, ed. C. Mayer (Basel: Schwabe, 2004).

Boulding, Maria. 'St Augustine's View of the Psalms as a Communion of Faith between Generations', *The Downside Review* 126 (2008): 128.

Brachtendorf, Johannes. *Die Struktur des menschlichen Geistes nach Augustinus: Selbstreflexion und Erkenntnis Gottes in* De Trinitate. Hamburg: Felix Meiner, 2000.

Brown, Peter. *Augustine of Hippo*. Los Angeles: University of California Press, 2000.

Brunning, Bernard and Anthony Dupont. 'To Be or Not to Be the Same, That is the Question: the Augustinian *Idipsum* as the Hinge between Two Modes of Being, the Divine and the Human', in *Studies in Spirituality* 31 (2021).

Cardó, Daniel. *The Cross and the Eucharist in Early Christianity: A Theological and Liturgical Investigation*. Cambridge: Cambridge University Press, 2019.

Cavadini, John C. 'The Darkest Enigma: Reconsidering the Self in Augustine's Thought', *Augustinian Studies* 38, no. 1 (2007): 119–32.

Clark, Mary T. 'Image Doctrine', in *Augustine through the Ages: An Encyclopedia*, ed. Allan Fitzgerald, 440–2. Grand Rapids: Eerdmans Publishing Company, 1999.

Dodaro, Robert. *Christ and the Just Society in the Thought of Augustine*. Cambridge: Cambridge University Press, 2004.

Drever, Matthew. *Image, Identity, and the Forming of the Augustinian Soul*. Oxford: Oxford University Press, 2013.

Drever, Matthew. 'Redeeming Creation: *Creatio ex nihilo* and the *Imago Dei* in Augustine', *International Journal of Systematic Theology* 15, no. 2 (2013): 135–53.

Drever, Matthew. 'Reimagining Human Personhood within the Body of Christ', *Augustinian Studies* 48, nos 1–2 (2017): 73–91.
Drever, Matthew. 'The Self Before God? Rethinking Augustine's Trinitarian Thought', *Harvard Theological Review* 100, no. 2 (2007): 233–42.
Falque, Emmanuel. *Dieu, la chair et l'autre: d'Irénée à Duns Scot*. Paris: Presses universitaires de France, 2008.
Falque, Emmanuel. *God, the Flesh and the Other: From Iraneus to Duns Scotus*. Evanston: Northwestern University Press, 2014.
Fiedrowicz, Michael. *Psalmus vox totius Christi. Studien zu Augustins Enarrationes in Psalmos*. Freiburg: Herder, 1997.
Giraud, Vincent. '*Signum* et *vestigium* dans la pensée de saint Augustin', *Revue des sciences philosophiques et théologiques* 5, no. 2 (2011): 251–74.
Gramigna, Remo. *Augustine's Theory of Signs, Signification, and Lying*. Boston: Walter de Gruyter, 2020.
Griffin, Carl W. and David L. Paulsen. 'Augustine *and the* Corporeality *of* God', *The Harvard Theological Review* 95, no. 1 (2002): 97–118.
Guarino, Thomas G. *Vincent of Lérins and the Development of Christian Doctrine*. Grand Rapids: Baker Books, 2013.
Guitton, Jean. *Le temps de l'éternité chez Plotin et Saint Augustin*. Paris: Vrin, 2004.
Heijke, John. '*Imago Dei* in the Works of Saint Augustine (Exclusive of *De trinitate*)', *Folia*, Special Supplemnet (1956).
Irizar, Pablo. 'Epistemología y Exégesis en las primeras obras de Agustín (387–391). Un análisis cronológico-temático de la palabra imago', *Augustinus* 63, no. 2 (2018): 417–44.
Irizar, Pablo. 'La cambiante interpretación literal de *imago Dei* en el joven Agustín (387–391): ¿dónde está la *imago Dei*, en el cuerpo o en el alma?' *Ciudad de Dios: Revista agustiniana* 229, no. 1 (2016): 27–53.
Irizar, Pablo. 'Sensing Dislocated Belonging: Augustine on Becoming Members of the Church as Images of God in the Expositions on the Psalms,' *Studies in Spirituality* 31, (2021), in press.
Irizar, Pablo. 'Scriptural Exegesis or Speculative Philosophy: Augustine on the Figure of the Cross as a Paradigm of Manifestation,' NZSTh 2021; 63(3): 1–24.
Irizar, Pablo. 'Where Is the Church? Augustine on Belonging as Unbound Images of God in the Church', *Louvain Studies* 44, no. 4 (2020).
Irizar, Pablo and Anthony Dupont. 'Many as One: Augustine's Onefold Ecclesiology', *International Journal of Philosophy and Theology*, forthcoming 2020.
Larmirande, Emilien. 'Note-Supplément bibliographique sur l'ecclésiologie de saint Augustin', *Revue d'Etudes Augustiniennes et Patristiques* 17 (1971): 177–82.

Larmirande, Emilien. 'Un siècle et demi d'études sur l'ecclésiologie de saint Augustin. Essai bibliographique', *Revue d'Etudes Augustiniennes et Patristiques* 8 (1962): 1–125.
Marion, Jean-Luc. 'Idipsum: The Name of God according to Augustine', in *Orthodox Readings of Augustine*, eds. George Demacopoulos and Aristotle Papanikolaou, 167–89. Crestwood: St. Vladimir's Seminary Press, 2008.
Marion, Jean-Luc. 'Notes sur l'usage de *substantia* par saint Augustin et sur son appartenance à l'histoire de la métaphysique', in *Mots médiévaux offerts à Ruedi Imbach*, eds. I. Atucha, D. Calma, C. König-Pralong and I. Zavatter. Porto: Fédération internationale des Instituts d'études médiévales, 2011.
Markus, Robert A. '*imago* and *similitudo* in Augustine', *Revue d'Etudes Augustiniennes et Patristiques* 10, nos 2–3 (1964): 125–43.
May, Gerhard. *The Doctrine of 'Creation out of Nothing' in Early Christian Thought*. Edinburgh: T&T Clark, 1994.
McCarthy, Michael C. 'An Ecclesiology of Groaning: Augustine, the Psalms, and the Making of Church', *Theological Studies* 66 (2005): 23–48.
O'Meara, John J. *The Creation of Man in St. Augustine's De Genesi ad litteram*. Villanova: Villanova Press, 1980.
Sullivan, John E. *The Image of God: The Doctrine of St. Augustine and Its Influence*. Dubuque: The Priory, 1963.
Teske, Roland. 'The Image and Likeness of God in St. Augustine's *De Genesi ad litteram liber imperfectus*', *Augustinianum* 30 (1990): 441–51.
Teske, Roland J. *Paradoxes of Time in Saint Augustine*. Marquette: Marquette University Press, 1996.
Torchia, Joseph. *Creatio ex nihilo and the Theology of St. Augustine: The Anti-Manichaean Polemic and Beyond*. New York: Peter Lang, 1999.
Welz, Claudia. *Humanity in God's Image: An Interdisciplinary Exploration*. Oxford: Oxford University Press, 2016.
Williams, Rowan. 'Augustine and the Psalms,' *Interpretation* 58, no. 1 (2004): 17–27.
Wisse, Maarten. *Trinitarian Theology beyond Participation: Augustine's De Trinitate and Contemporary Theology*. London: T&T Clark, 2011.
Zwollo, Laela. *St. Augustine and Plotinus: The Human Mind as Image of the Divine*. Leiden: Brill, 2018.

INDEX

1 Cor 11.7   26

absence   1–3, 7, 9, 10, 14, 18, 29–31, 33, 35, 37, 54, 57, 59, 78, 79, 82, 103, 114, 116, 117, 126, 127, 130, 131
alterity   4–7, 10, 11, 15, 16, 19, 20, 22, 26–43, 45, 46, 49–56, 59, 78, 126
Aristotle   38, 43–9

body   xi, xii, 4–8, 24–7, 30, 37, 46, 47, 51–4, 56, 57, 59, 65–78, 81–96, 98, 99, 102, 103, 107, 109, 116, 120, 123, 126, 127, 129, 131

capax dei   43, 46
categories   2, 38, 44–6, 48
Christ   x, xi, xii, 3, 6–8, 18, 19, 21–5, 28, 29, 37, 38, 49–52, 54–7, 59, 60, 63, 65–79, 81, 89, 94–104, 108, 112, 118, 126, 127, 129, 131
church   viii, ix, x, xi, xii, 1–9, 25, 30, 37, 39, 50–2, 55–7, 59, 60, 63, 65–7, 69–79, 81, 82, 89, 94, 95, 98–103, 125–31
City of God   21, 30, 41, 43, 95
Col 1.15   19
community   x, xi, xii, 1–3, 7, 39, 51, 54, 55, 60, 99–101, 103, 130, 131

Confessions   3–6, 12, 19, 25, 28, 42, 43, 60, 62, 94, 106, 109, 114, 116, 118

deconfinement   xiii, 8, 103, 126, 128, 130, 131
de nihilo   20, 21, 29, 30
difference   5, 6, 9–11, 15–23, 26, 28, 29, 31–43, 45–7, 49, 53, 56, 114, 122, 126, 127
dyadic   10, 15, 21, 28, 38, 39, 41–3, 51, 126

Easter   xiii, 6, 8, 128, 130
Eph 3.18   88, 89, 95–7, 99
Ex 3.14   134, 136
ex nihilo   20, 21, 25, 85

falsehood   14–18, 21, 24, 27, 30, 31, 41–3, 45

gaze   7, 8, 60, 89, 106, 123, 125
Gen 1.26   13, 15, 19, 22, 23, 25, 26
God   7, 8, 12, 13, 18–25, 27–34, 37–46, 48–57, 60, 62, 64, 66, 67, 69, 73, 75–7, 82–6, 88, 89, 93–102, 105–12, 116–19, 122, 125–31

heart   2, 4, 5, 18, 25, 27, 28, 31, 41, 50, 51, 60, 63, 71, 72, 99, 100, 107

INDEX

identity   5, 6, 9–19, 21–38, 42, 43, 53, 56, 68–70, 101, 126
idipsum   6, 20, 28, 33, 34, 110
image   2, 10–29, 32–4, 38–43, 50–7, 61, 65, 73, 89, 91, 96, 102, 113, 121, 123, 126
invisibility   7, 8, 77, 79, 81–5, 89, 99, 103, 104, 126, 127, 130, 131

Jn 19.26   70
Jn 19.28   70
Jn 19.30   68
Jn 20.27   134

likeness   6, 10, 13–25, 28–35, 39–42, 48, 52, 53, 121
Lk 18.41   134
Lk 23.34   70, 101
Lk 23.43   70
Lk 23.46   70, 77
Lk 24.39   134
love   x, xi, xii, xiii, xiv, 3–5, 11, 13, 40, 41, 49–51, 60–3, 66, 96, 99, 100, 106, 109, 125

manifestation   3, 7, 8, 21, 25, 28, 34, 50, 51, 54, 57, 60, 75, 77, 81–3, 85, 86, 88, 89, 92, 94–100, 103, 104, 107–9, 114, 123, 127, 131
Matt 26.41   134, 148
Matt 27.46   70
metamorphosis   105, 107, 112, 114, 115, 119, 121–4, 127
Mk 15.34   70, 101
music   62, 63, 84, 109, 110, 112–15, 117–23
mystery   6, 21, 32, 38, 65, 76, 78, 89, 95, 97–9, 101, 109, 131

ontology   13–19, 22, 24, 27, 29, 30, 38, 40, 79, 86, 126

pandemic   viii, x, xi, xii, 1, 3, 5, 7–10, 35, 37, 81, 82, 105, 125, 127, 128, 130, 131
paradox   4, 10, 18, 19, 24, 26, 28–33, 35, 36, 62, 65, 69, 70, 99, 108–13, 118, 122, 126
Paul   4, 12, 18, 19, 21, 22, 29, 67, 76, 77, 97, 109, 123, 126, 129
Plato   6, 13–15, 17, 19–22, 24, 25, 28–30, 32, 33, 42, 83, 111, 126
Psalm   3, 4, 6, 51, 55, 59, 63–70, 75, 78, 110

sacrament   viii, x, xii, 1–3, 77, 78, 96, 99, 121, 128, 129, 131
se cogitare   42
selfsame   110
se nosse   42
separation   xii, 4–6, 9, 66, 78, 101, 127, 128, 130
sign   11, 12, 15, 31, 37, 53, 82, 89–99, 101–3, 108, 113, 114, 126, 131

time   x, xi, xii, xiii, xiv, 3–5, 7–9, 11, 15, 21, 28–30, 32, 33, 35, 38, 42, 47, 50, 56, 63, 66, 68, 73–6, 85, 94, 104–6, 108–24, 128–31
Trinity   15, 20, 22, 27–9, 33, 34, 36–49, 51, 55, 56, 60, 77, 87, 92, 126
truth   6, 10, 13–19, 21–5, 30, 33, 35, 39, 41–5, 60, 62, 63, 65, 67, 70–2, 77, 78, 83–5, 95, 109, 114, 115, 121, 130

Whole Christ   56, 57, 59, 65, 71, 73, 74, 76, 103